# Living
# In the Word

### A 90 Day Walk In God's Word

By Ron Barnett

Copyright © 2012 Ron Barnett

All rights reserved.

**ISBN-13:** 978-1478220749
**ISBN-10:** 1478220740

# DEDICATION

This book is dedicated to my Lord and Savior Jesus Christ who saved me and inspired me as to what to write and to my wife Beth, who gave me the confidence to write when I wasn't sure I could.

## ACKNOWLEGDEMEMNTS

To Cassie Moore:
Without your help, this book would not have been possible. Thanks for finding my mistakes and fixing them.

To my family and friends:
You encouraged me and gave me your support. You will never know how much that has meant to me.

# PREFACE

Dear Reader,

Several years ago, I began to write a weekly devotional that I sent to members of our church along with friends and family all over the country. Without fail, each week the Lord brought to my mind a scripture, along with a story to share with the people of God. Over the years, I received several positive responses, as people told me how the Weekly Word had spoken to them about their lives. I was encouraged to put them together into book form and make it available to the Christian community at large. The book you are holding is a compilation of those writings. It is my hope that it will inspire you, instruct you, and challenge you to follow closely to God, learn his ways, and apply his word to your everyday life. If after following this 90 day excursion, you find yourself in a more intimate, loving, life-changing relationship with Jesus, this book and the message it conveys will have accomplished the goal we originally envisioned for it. So get started, and see where the Lord takes you as you devote yourself to him.

Yours In Christ,

Ron Barnett

# DAY ONE

## Everyday Joy

Terry had always been a man who was full of life. For those of you who knew him, he was great with people of all ages, but especially the very young. Terry was no buffoon. He was a serious businessman and a leader that people followed, respected and admired. He had the unique ability to relate to people, specifically children. Little kids loved him and he loved them. He would see a young child in church or at the store and begin to talk to them, laugh with them and generally have a good time. He had a charm and an ease with people while still possessing the ability to be silly. To many kids, it was if he were a little kid wrapped up in an adult body. The image that summed up his life best was while he was making his way across the parking lot of a restaurant one Mothers' Day holding hands with his two granddaughters on either side of him. Spontaneously, the two 5-year-old girls decided they wanted to skip to the car, and so, their grandfather decided that he would skip too. It was an image of pure, unrestrained joy that refused to worry about what others might think, and the thought of it still makes some laugh to this day.

For the Christ-follower, this image of joy should not be foreign. Though we live in a world of pressure; pressure to perform, to get results, and even to survive, we cannot allow that pressure to hamper our ability to laugh, love, and genuinely enjoy life. We must never allow the stresses we face to rob us of our ability to be silly or spontaneous. And while God's desire for us it not to ignore the seriousness of the issue encounter, we must never allow those issues to overtake us and become a roadblock to our happiness. The Psalm-writer explains that God has "turned for me my mourning into dancing. You have put off my sackcloth and clothed me with gladness" (Psalm 30:11). As we walk closely with God, we can face pressure with a smile and manage the stresses of life with a song in our hearts. Are you enjoying life or merely enduring it? Have you lost your ability to be glad, your power to be joyful, your capacity to be silly? Call out to God. He will trade your sorrows for joy, and your pain for peace and happiness. Before you know it, you may even feel like skipping.

## DAY TWO

### If Only

Ben had made some really bad choices in his life. He had done some things as a young man, that later in life, left him with many regrets. And as the consequences of a life spent making bad choices came full circle, he spent his days beating himself up and wishing he could undo the mistakes of his past. Though he could do nothing to erase what had taken place, he found himself tempted to utter the most useless and even damaging phrase in the English language, "If only". If only I had done things differently, he thought. If only I would have paid more attention to this or that. If only I had chosen this path over that one, my life would have turned out differently and potentially better. As he picked up the pieces of his broken life, he realized could use his experiences to glean insight on how to prepare for a brighter future for himself. Though endlessly reviewing all the missteps of his youth would do him no good, his misfortunes might actually help him in helping others. Even though he couldn't change the events of the past, he could affect the future for himself, as well as someone else.

The Bible tells us that the "steps of a righteous man are ordered of God" (Psalm 37:23) and that everything, even the bad decisions of our past can "work together for good to those who love the Lord and are called according to His purpose" (Romans 8:28). God even goes so far as to tell us that He has plans for us, "plans to prosper you and not to harm you, so that you may have a future and a hope." (Jeremiah 29:11) It is not God's desire to dictate the details of our lives according to some cosmic formula. He has given us the freedom to choose our destiny and our fate, knowing that we will make some mistakes along the way. But even when mistakes happen, we can be assured that He able to not only help us correct them but use them, for His glory and our good. Is your life filled with regrets? Do you look back and see the times that things could have been different if only you had known? Make a vow today to quit reliving the disappointments of the past and start following the plans of the Lord today. If we do, He will direct our paths to future victory in this life and the life to come.

## DAY THREE

### God And The Green Crayon

Jessica was getting her son ready to start his first day of kindergarten. She obtained a list of necessary supplies from the school and had gone to the local store to fill the list. Later at home, as she was checking off each item and placing it into her son's back pack, the boy was looking over all his new supplies with excitement. As he opened his new box of 16 crayons, he discovered that the green one was broken. Concerned and distraught at his discovery, he desperately showed his mother the horrible sight. From his childlike perspective he was devastated, certain that his first day of school was now ruined beyond repair. As Jessica dried her son's tears, she reassured him that the crayon company was busy working seven days a week doing nothing but making crayons. She went on to explain that the store where they had purchased the crayons was open twenty-four hours a day and to obtain a completely new box of crayons would only cost $1.39. What had seemed like an insurmountable problem with no hope of a solution to her little boy was really a simple problem with an even simpler solution to her.

Often times, if we are not careful, we approach God with our problems like the boy in the story. Because we cannot see a solution, we assume that there is none. We cry, and fret, and stew in our difficulties convinced that there is no hope because the answer to our dilemma eludes us. But like Jessica, God caringly reassures us that our perspective is limited while His is limitless. The Bible tells us that "God will meet all your needs according to the riches of his glory." (Philippians 4:19) God does not expect us to meet all of our needs with the resources that we have at our disposal, because eventually they will run out. We must remember that our needs are met by the One, whose perspective is infinite and eternal and whose resources are endless. Are you upset over difficulties that seem insurmountable? Do you try to meet your own needs only to come up short? God is the perfect parent and, if we allow Him, He will share with us His perspective, and His resources, and will lead us along every step of the path of life.

## DAY FOUR

### From Change To Real Money

Just inside the front door of Linda's house, just past the coat rack, right next to the umbrella tree was a large jar where Linda kept spare change. At the end of each day, she would deposit the fractured fragments of what used to be ones, fives, tens and twenties and place them into the container. Periodically, when the container was full, Linda would take the coinage somewhere to be counted and mysteriously, almost magically, converted back into more practical currency. Almost without exception, it amazed her how much was there. She was flabbergasted as to how much good could come from something that was, up to that point, leftover and virtually useless. With this change she saved for vacations, made significant donations to charity, and even helped send a young person from her church on a missions trip to South America. All that from change collected over time; from what most of us would consider scraps of money that are rather worthless and undesirable.

God does a similar work in the life of the believer. Most of the time, when we come to God, it is with the fractured fragments of our lives in our hands. We assess our situation and determine that our lives are a waste and no good thing could come from us. We are left with only the parts that others have discarded, the rejected pieces that no one else would want. But when we present those pieces to God, He takes them and somehow makes something good out of it. Jesus told his disciples; when feeding a large group of people to "Gather the pieces that are left over. Let nothing be wasted." (John 6:12) In a process that still astounds us, God can assembles our excess pieces and fashions something beautiful and valuable with them, restoring us to our former splendor. We marvel at His handiwork and wonder how so much good could come from the leftover and the useless things of our lives. Do you feel rejected and discarded today? Do you feel like you life is full of leftovers, like all you have are fragments of a real life? Bring your excess pieces to God and He will mold them into something useful and beautiful again.

DAY FIVE

**What's The Difference?**

At age seven, Bobby never liked going to the dentist. Between the drills and the x-rays, the whole idea did not appeal to him. But he did like the children's magazines he found in the waiting room. One in particular contained a puzzle that involved two pictures. The children were challenged to find the differences in two seemingly identical pictures. Bobby would stare intently at the one picture, trying to memorize every line and form, then stare at the other, looking hard for something to be out of place. Within just a few minutes, he would see the man in one picture with a hat on had none in the other. Or the woman with a baby carriage who was standing far away from the tree in the first picture was somehow standing right next to it in the other. Though the differences were subtle, each picture was distinct enough to notice that they were not the same.

As Christ-followers, like the pictures in the children's magazine, we are called to be different than the world around us. Though we may look very similar to those we meet each day, we are called to live a life that makes us unique and sets us apart from the status quo. If we have been touched by the power of God, if we order our lives according to His precepts and teachings; we have no choice but to be different. Our actions and attitudes will be Christ-centered and not follow the patterns of the world. While we cannot assume that we are better than anyone, we must live a life worthy of a relationship with Almighty God. The Apostle Peter reminds us that we "are a chosen people, a royal priesthood, a holy nation, a people belonging to God." (1 Peter 2:9) While we are called to live in a world where Godliness is not the standard, interacting daily with those around us who may not share our perspective, we must continue to strive to exhibit Christ-like character in our attitudes and actions. Have you embraced the fact that God has called you to live differently? Or are you striving to be just like everyone else? Like Moses who came down from the mountain after a close encounter with the Almighty, as we draw close to God, the world around us will notice the difference in us, not merely on the outside, but on the inside where it counts.

## DAY SIX

### Follow Close

John decided to move with his family across the country in search of new opportunities. Excited about their journey, they packed the moving truck with all their belongings and said goodbye to their family and friends as they set out on their new adventure. John drove the moving truck, while his wife and their oldest daughter would follow him in their cars. They would create their own caravan down the highway as they made their way to their new home. Since none of them had driven that far before, John pulled the team together for some last-minute instructions. He told his family, "Follow me, wherever I go. Stay close behind me and everything will be alright". The family followed his instructions and stayed close, making it all the way to their destination safe and sound.

John's instructions are the same words that the Jesus said to the disciples as he called them. He said "Come, follow me" (Matthew 4:19). They are the same words that He says to you and I, as we journey through our Christian life. While we can be sure of our final destination, we may not always be sure of the twist and turns that will arise along the way. But no matter where we find ourselves, we can be confident that if we follow Him, we will arrive safely. The key to following God, like following anyone else, is to stay close. If we allow too much space to occur, it is possible to lose sight of Him in the hectic traffic of life and find ourselves lost and alone. Have you lost your way? Are you trying to navigate through this life on your own? Stay close to God and He will guide you through and get you to your new home in heaven safe and sound.

## DAY SEVEN

### New Beach Everyday

From body surfing to splashing in the waves to just relaxing by the ocean, there was nothing that Amy didn't like about the beach. She had always thought it was a great place to spend a day. As she sat in her chair soaking up the sun, she loved to watch her four kids build sand castles. Some of their designs were amazing. While some kids just liked to dig big holes, leaving the sand looking like a team of gophers had made a summer home there, her kids liked to build structures on the beach. Each was a marvel of engineering including towers and walls with gates and the occasional moat for protection. Amy liked the intricate structures that took time, and energy, and demonstrated her kids' burgeoning creativity, she also like that it kept them occupied while she relaxed on the shore. Her kids always thought that building sand castles was great fun, but they soon realized that even the most intricate structures were temporary at best. Eventually the tides would come ashore, flattening the castle and filling in the holes, leaving the beach looking exactly like it did before anyone arrived. It's as though each day, the waves of the ocean erase the previous day and, every morning, the beach is made brand new.

The Bible tells us that the mercies of the Lord "are new every morning" (Lamentation 3:23). Like the waves of the sea that remove the previous day's activity from the sand of the beach, God's mercies rush in and make it so that every day can be a new start. Each day, we have the opportunity to be remade, fresh and clean, with the holes filled in and shaky structures of yesterday washed away. As we reach out to God, the tide of his love and care washes over us and makes us new. Do you need your beach cleared? Do you feel like yesterday is crowding out today? Call out to God and earnestly ask Him to make you new. You'll be surprised what a clean start will do for you.

LIFE LESSON IN THE WORD

## DAY EIGHT

### Be Bold

Paige had always been somewhat timid. In a group, while others seemed to want to dominate the conversation, she was quite content to sit back and watch. Rather intimidated, she was unsure whether her opinions would be accepted by other, more outspoken, people. That's what made her actions in the office that day seem all the more strange. Marge, the lady at the next desk, was checking her email when she came across one from a company that she had never heard of offering her a $10,000 shopping spree for just answering a few questions. All she had to do was click on the link in the email and she would be asked a series of consumer questions that qualified her for the prize. As Marge read the email aloud, Paige realized that it was a scam. Her mother had fallen for the same thing just a week before. There was no prize and clicking on the link released a virus that would destroy the computer's hard drive. Without thinking, Paige shouted, "Don't do it Marge!" Everyone in the office looked at Paige in astonishment, not only for the fact that she saved Marge's computer, but that she spoke so boldly and forcefully to prevent what could have been a difficult situation.

Oftentimes, we as disciples of Christ, are hesitant to share our faith. Like Paige, we may be concerned that we will offend someone or that they will not accept us. In Acts 3, a story is told of Peter and John and their encounter with a lame man at the temple gate. They had no money to give him but, through the power of God, they were able to heal him. This set off a firestorm of controversy with the Jewish leaders and Peter and John were brought in to give an account for their actions. As Peter spoke, the religious leaders "saw the boldness of Peter and John and realized that they were unschooled, ordinary men, they were astonished and they took note that these men had been with Jesus." (Acts 4:13) Boldness is uncommon courage due to uncommon insight. As the Sanhedrin examined the source of the disciples' boldness, they determined it was not from any special education or training, nor was it from any extraordinary ability. They determined that their courage came from insight they had gleaned from spending time with Jesus. Are you inhibited about sharing your faith? Are you afraid that you don't have what it takes? Spend time with Jesus and He will give you wisdom and insight that will give you the boldness to speak up and make a difference in someone's life.

# DAY NINE

## Leafy Or Fruity

Those who knew Jonah best, knew that he was no good with plants. Every green thing he touched was soon to die. Yet despite his efforts, Jonah had a very large and bushy tree growing in his backyard. The tree had been there for years and grew larger and bushier every year. One fall day, Jonah decided to cut the tree back so that he could better mow the grass around it. The following spring as he was doing yard work, he noticed that the tree had sprouted little green spheres about the size of golf balls. Jonah determined that his tree must be some kind of fruit tree. So that fall, he cut the tree back even further in hopes of coaxing the tree to produce fruit. The following spring, he noticed large red fruit hanging from several branches. As it turned out, his tree was an apple tree. While it had been an apple tree all along, it had never produced any fruit. Though it was full of rich lush greenery, Jonah realized that the health of a fruit tree is not determined by how leafy it is but how much fruit it produces.

We as believers in Jesus are called to produce "the fruit of the Spirit."(Galatians 5:22) Like the branch of a fruit tree, we are all grafted into the main branch and allow the juices of power and life to produce fruit in us from the inside out. While there are some believers who try to make their trees look healthy with many leaves, the health of a tree is determined by its fruit, a fruit produced so that others can come and enjoy it. Are you producing fruit or just leaves? Are others able to enjoy the fruit that comes from you? Allow the Spirit of God to work on the inside of you and, before you know it, choice fruit will grow and those around you will be blessed.

## DAY TEN

### It's All In the Taste

Sandra had always wanted to cook. As a little girl, she had watched her mother in the kitchen working tirelessly on her culinary creations. She heard the "oohs" and "aah's of people who tasted her mother's cooking and had always enjoyed the food herself. Inspired by her mother's example, Sandra decided to make a special dinner for her mom's birthday, and whip up several of her favorite dishes. However what she thought would turn out wonderfully, only ended in disaster. The roast looked dry. The mashed potatoes were lumpy and the gravy runny. Even the cake that she had made for dessert had come out lopsided. Discouraged and on the verge of tears, Sandra went into the dining room to sulk. Just then, she heard a strange sound coming from the kitchen. She heard it again, "Ooh, that's good." As she peaked around the kitchen door, she saw her mother with a spoon in her hand tasting Sandra's work. She offered a spoonful to Sandra and told her to just try it. Though it didn't look very appealing, she had to admit it tasted pretty good. As she and her mother prepared the table for dinner, they both agreed that Sandra's food didn't look like much, but that it's really the taste that counts.

Some people resist following God wholeheartedly because the idea doesn't seem appealing to them. They are not sure what to make of God so they avoid following too closely for fear of what He will ask or what unseen ramifications might appear. But the Bible tells us clearly to "taste and see that the Lord is good." (Psalm 34:8) The promise is that if you and I will really submit ourselves to God, if we will simply "try" Him, we will find Him to be good and the sweetness of His countenance will be very appealing. The initial hesitancy and strangeness that kept us away from Him will quickly evaporate. Are you holding back from God because you're unsure of what total surrender will look like? Do you find God's appearance strange and, despite repeated appeals, you still resist? If we will but open ourselves to Him and just give God a try, we may find that He is surprisingly good, better that we could ever have hoped for.

## DAY ELEVEN

### Instant Cocoa

As Neil removed his cup from the microwave, he looked sadly at the brown liquid staring back at him, which was passing for hot cocoa. He remembered a time before many of the modern conveniences when hot chocolate was made the old fashioned way. His mom would heat a pan of milk on the stove. When the milk was just right, she would pour it into a mug, stir in a generous portion of chocolate syrup, and add two large marshmallows too finish it off. While the process took several minutes, there was nothing more satisfying than a creamy cup of chocolately goodness on a cold winter's day. Now, with the microwave as a staple in American kitchens, a less than adequate substitute has tried to replace the goodness of mom's hot chocolate using water, brown chocolate-flavored powder, and freeze dried marshmallows. While that mixture can be in a cup ready to drink in a matter of seconds, those who remember the original say that the taste is less than appealing. Even though there is a savings in time, the quality suffers under the pressure to hurry things along.

The same thing can be said in our daily experience with God. We hear the promises of God and suddenly we are in a rush to grasp them. We want to hurry the process along so that we can enjoy all the good things that we believe we deserve. While we want the good things that God has for us, we are often willing to trade quality for expediency, excellence for ease. But God will not allow us to cheat ourselves out of the blessing he has for us. God's timing is perfect. When He told his people in the desert that He would lead them into the promised-land, He told them that they would take the land "little by little."(Exodus 23:30) God's desire was not to frustrate them, but to teach the value of waiting and striving for the best instead of settling for the quick and easy. His plan for us is the same. His desire is to see us fulfill our destiny at a pace that will not overwhelm us but allow us to fully enjoy the richness of his blessings. Do you tend to get ahead of God? Do you want everything and want it now? We must be aware that God's goal for us is success and blessings, for which there is no shortcut. Trust God because His best for us is worth the wait.

## DAY TWELVE

## Good Thinking

Nicole liked it when her mother read her a story before bed each night. Though she had lots of story books, her favorite was the story of the Ugly Duckling. It is a fable about a swan that thinks he is a duck. In the story, the little swan does his best to be a good duck. Despite his best efforts, he never measures up. He is rejected by the other ducks, and made to feel inferior because he is different. Though he does his best to walk, talk, swim and act like a duck, his differences still show. Feeling out of place, he feels doomed to a life of misery because all the while, he thinks he is a duck. His whole life changed the day he realized he is a not a duck, but a graceful swan. Though nothing on the outside of him was different, with his perspective changed, he gained a new lease on life. It was what he believed about himself that made the difference.

Many followers of Jesus suffer from the same problem as the Ugly Duckling. They believe a lie about themselves and order their lives around it. And even though doing so brings them nothing but heartaches and headaches, they persist because they believe it is their lot in life. The Bible tells us that whatever a person "thinks in his heart, so is he." (Proverbs 23:7) We cannot always believe what popular culture says about us. Likewise, we cannot base our lives on the opinions of others. We cannot even always believe how we feel about ourselves. We must believe the word of God. Over and over, God tells us how precious we are to Him. His desire is that we develop meaning and fulfillment in life from your relationship with Him. Do you find yourself trying to live out an identity that doesn't seem to fit? Have you believed a lie about yourself? Look to God and His word and He will reshape your thinking so that you can live according to His view of you.

## DAY THIRTEEN

## **The Penny Principle**

Emily had always been careful with her money. As a young girl, her father taught her the value of a dollar. Now as a single woman out on her own, she wanted to be responsible and make him proud. One day as she was walking out of a pharmacy, she saw a penny on the ground. She noticed that several people had walked right by the copper coin, paying no attention to it lying on the pavement. Other people had seen it but must have determined it wasn't worth the effort. As she made his way over to it, she saw another person look down at it and start to pick it up, only to realize that it was only a penny and continue on their way. Quietly she made her way over to it, picked it up and took it home to add to the collection of coins she kept in a jar by her bed. Her father taught her that if she would keep track of the pennies, the dollars will take care of themselves; if she would see the value in each penny and collect them, before long, she will be rich.

Jesus told a story of a man who was treated much like the penny. He was traveling from Jerusalem to Jericho when he "fell into the hands of robbers". (Luke 10:30) They took everything he had, beat him and left him for dead. Many people walked by the man laying there and didn't even notice him. Two different religious people saw him, and determining that he had no significance to them, crossed the street to avoid him. Finally, a Good Samaritan came along and helped the beaten man, taking time and energy to value him as another human being. Jesus indicated that the Good Samaritan was the only person in the story who acted rightly. He was the only one who treated the broken man the way God would. Are you too busy to see those in need around you? Have you overlooked as unimportant what God values most? Take time today to treasure the "pennies" you encounter each day and before long, you may be surprised how rich you really are.

# DAY FOURTEEN

## Margin Call

All Adam wanted to do was make good grades in college. As the first in his family to ever have the ability to attend, he was humbled by the sacrifice his parents were making to give him this chance. At the same time, he also felt a deep sense of responsibility not to waste this precious opportunity. When he got to the bookstore to buy his books, he was overwhelmed by how expensive everything was. With the cost of books so high, he would have to cut back on other supplies like paper for taking notes. Adam noticed wide margins in many his books, so as classes began, he decided to take notes there. He thought it would not only save on paper but keep needed information together and make studying for test a breeze. Adam couldn't have been more wrong. Book publishers put margins around the text of a book to create breathing space for the reader. They have found that a cramped page makes it hard for readers to concentrate on the text and to find things later should the need arise. Adam soon found the same thing. When he went to study for his first exam, he couldn't make heads or tails of what was on each page. Though he struggled to make a C on his exams, he learned a valuable lesson. Cluttering up the margins can only lead to disaster.

God has set up the world and everything in it to run on margins as well. But in the hectic pace of our busy world, our schedules get so full that it seems that every minute of our lives is consumed in some activity. Soon, our margins are full and things quickly get out of balance. Then, what was designed to work in harmony is soon headed for disaster. God has set out the guidelines for these natural margins in His word. In it He gave his people a commandment designed to keep their lives in balance. "Six days you will work and on the seventh day you will rest." (Exodus 23:12) God gave this command not to create workplace disharmony but to help His people strike a balance between the responsibilities of providing for their families and their responsibilities to honor the God who created them and provided for them. If we will learn to maintain God's blueprint for balance in our lives, we will be more productive than if we ignore his plan. Have you begun to fill up the margins in your life? Has your breathing space become cluttered and stuffy? If we will observe the precepts regarding setting proper margins, we will not only fulfill the daily requirements of our lives, but maintain order and balance along the way.

## DAY FIFTEEN

### What's Eating You?

Joel had always been a nice guy. His parents had taught him to live by "The Golden Rule" and he genuinely tried to treat everyone the way he would want to be treated. He ran into his biggest challenge when he met Dorothy. Joel's boss had retired and Dorothy was promoted to be his new supervisor. Others who had worked with her cautioned Joel that she was a tough manager and, at times, impossible to please, but he was determined not to prejudge her. During their first staff meeting, he knew he was in for a challenge. Dorothy spoke to everyone in gruff tones, barking out orders like a drill sergeant. She was abrupt with people to the point of being rude and highly critical of everyone's work. Despite all that, Joel still tried to do his best to be pleasant around her. Then one day, he checked his email only to find a sarcastic note. Dorothy was questioning the work he had done on the latest project, and insulting his ability and his intellect. For Joel, that was more than enough. As his anger boiled and his face grew hot, he marched down the hall to Dorothy's office determined to clear the air with her. As he reached her door, he could see she was on the phone. While he waited furiously outside, he overheard a conversation with her son begging him not to move away and take her grandkids from her. She pleaded for another chance to a make their relationship right, but he hung up on her. As he peaked around the office door, and saw that she had been crying, Joel's heart broke. Dorothy had not been difficult because she wanted to be. The pain she was experiencing in her personal life was spilling over to those in the business world.

From time to time we all run into difficult people. Whether at school or in the workplace or even at home, we deal with someone whose painful circumstances cause them to create pain in the lives of others. Even though it is difficult, Jesus commands his followers to "love your enemies and pray for those who persecute you, that you may be children of your Father in heaven." (Matthew 5:44-45) God knows that we cannot manufacture this kind of love from within ourselves. It is only as we allow God to help us that we can be a channel of His love to the demanding people around us. Are you dealing with a difficult person? Can you look past their rough exterior to their inner pain? God wants to use His children to represent Him to a hurting world. We are never more like our heavenly Father than when we love others, no matter how unlovable.

## DAY SIXTEEN

## Meaningless To Meaningful

Karen had always searched for meaning in her life. She first sought fame believing that if only she could attain some notoriety and be the center of everyone's attention, she would find happiness. But fame is hard to attain and ever harder to keep. It quickly fades, leaving hopes dashed along with a sense of emptiness. Next she sought meaning in accomplishments, expecting that will make her happy. After she had reached the summit of many of her goals, she found there were no more mountains to climb and no new challenges to sustain her. She next tried to gather wealth under the assumption that having all she wanted would bring contentment. Unfortunately she soon found that the desire for more never really goes away no matter how much we acquire. She then sought meaning in relationships, hopping from one person to another in hopes of finding a special someone who will meet all her needs, only to realize that no one is perfect and all relationships require work. After all her best efforts; after striving, searching, working and wanting, she still found herself in need of satisfaction and fulfillment.

No one knew the meaninglessness of striving more than King Solomon, the wisest and richest man of his day. He had more, knew more, loved more, and was idolized more than anyone in the world. Yet he wrote in the book of Ecclesiastes that "everything is meaningless" (Ecclesiastes 1:2) Over eleven chapters he surveys relationships, accomplishment, fame and fortune, finding all of them meaningless. Finally, at the end of his book, he settles on "the conclusion of the matter: Fear God and keep his commandments."(Ecclesiastes 12:13) The wisest man to ever live proclaimed that following God is the only source of lasting satisfaction. Are you striving for something only to fall short? Have you put your efforts into pursuing happiness that won't last? Start investing yourself in earnestly following after God and you will find contentment that nothing else can match.

## DAY SEVENTEEN

### God's Pain Reliever

Alan woke up in the morning with a headache. His head throbbed as he got dressed and the pain only intensified as he made his way downstairs for breakfast. He shuffled into the kitchen and looked at his wife through eyes that were only partially open. As she handed him his coffee, she suggested that pain reliever might alleviate his aching head, but he ignored her. He hated to take pills so he determined that his was something he would just have to endure. What Alan failed to understand was that while pain relievers can clear up the chronic aches and pains we experience, just having pain reliever in the house does us no good. Taking the jar of pills out of the cabinet and placing them on a table will still not bring relief. Taking the tablets out of the bottle and holding them in our hands will prove unrewarding as well. We can even rub them on the source of our pain but nothing will change. Only when we take the pain reliever internally and give it some time to work will it go to the source of our pain and alleviate our discomfort. While most of us are unsure as to how the medicine works or how it knows where the pain is, we are confident that given the opportunity to work, our pain will eventually subside.

The word of God in our lives is much like a pain reliever. Many people have a Bible in their house, but have no peace. They may have it displayed where they can see it in times of stress, yet it will still do them no good. Only when we take the word of God into our lives and internalize its message will we find relief for the chronic pain we often experience. While most of us are unsure as to how it works or how it can find the problem areas of our lives, we can be confident that given the opportunity to work, our pain will subside and we will find rest for our souls. In his word, God tells us not to "merely listen to the word, and so deceive yourselves. Do what it says."(James 1:22) Are you suffering with pain that could be avoided? Are you desperate to find relief but don't know where to looks? Let the message of God's word move past the surface of your life? Take it internally and watch it bring health and wholeness to your entire being.

## DAY EIGHTEEN

## Advertising Jesus

As a copywriter for an ad agency, Andrea knew her job was to put the best face possible on products in the hope that the people would buy it. So each ad she put together, whether radio, television, or billboard was about telling all the wonderful aspects of her client's product. To do this, she used attractive people in interesting and exotic locales. She wanted them to exude happiness and joy when discussing the wonderful things this product has done for them and how it has added something positive in their lives. Andrea knew that advertisers don't pay large sums of money to produce commercials and distribute their message with people who don't look happy about their product. That would be a waste of time, money and energy. Advertisers don't want people to believe negative things about their product, but want to show it in the most positive light possible.

As Christ-followers, we are walking, breathing advertisements for Jesus. Our faces are the billboards that people read to determine whether our walk with God is something that they would like to try. The Bible tells us to "Rejoice in the Lord and be glad." (Psalm 32:11) The root word of rejoice is the word "Joy", which is defined as "an outward show of pleasure or delight". We as believers are called to spread the joy of our salvation wherever we are. Yet, some walk around with a sour expression and an even more sorrowful disposition and wonder why people aren't lined up to follow their God. Do you need to spruce up your billboard? Are you a showing Jesus in the most positive light possible? Remember today that people are watching you and, while God does not expect us to be perfect, He does ask us to be as consistently joyous as we can.

## DAY NINETEEN

## **Solid Or Sandy?**

Barbara had lived in the same house for the last 42 years. Though she had remained a fixture in the community, everything around her had changed. The people in the houses on her street had changed several times over the years. The Parkers had been her next door neighbors since 1978, but after her husband died, Evelyn sold her house to a developer who had knocked it down to build a brand new house on the same lot. It seemed to Barbara that nothing ever stayed the same and everything in the world was always changing. The news that her best friend from high school had just died of cancer left her even more uneasy. Even the familiar things in her life seemed different. Though she had been there her whole life, she barely recognized most of the people at her church. The ones she had known had either died or moved away and the whole place was full of new and unfamiliar faces. And though she loved it when her grandkids came over to see her, they too were changing. If they weren't making fun of her vintage television that only got four channels, they had their faces buried in the latest gadgets and gizmos. While Barbara knew that times and people both change, she longed for something substantial, something solid she could hold onto in the midst of the whirlwind of change that swirled around her.

Jesus understands this need in the human heart for something secure to hold on to when life all around us seems unstable. He told His followers that "everyone who hears these words of mine and puts them into practice is like a wise man who built his house on the rock." (Matthew 7:24) Jesus explained that, oftentimes, the world around us can grow erratic and unpredictable, but if we build on the solid foundation of His word, everything will come out the other side unharmed. On the other hand, if we ignore the words of Jesus, if we choose to build our house on a foundation of shifting sand. Even the smallest breath of wind or slightest change in circumstances will lead to massive devastation and difficulty. Does the world around you seem like sinking sand? Do you need something rock-solid on which you can depend? Build your life on the steadiness found in God's word and even as the world around you changes, you will be secure, not only today, but tomorrow and for the rest of your life.

## DAY TWENTY

### God's Traffic Signals

Garrett hated to wait. It seemed that every time he was in a hurry to get somewhere, he would get caught in traffic lights; lights that seemed to last forever. Though he was impatient, Garrett knew that crossing a street or driving through an intersection could be very hazardous if not done at the proper time. Traffic signals, no matter how annoying, make it possible for people to navigate the streets of any city safely by regulating the timing each group of people is allowed to be in the interception. Oftentimes, it not is a given action that is dangerous, but the timing of it that can lead to success or failure. Even though sitting at a red light waiting for traffic to clear can be bothersome, it is far better than venturing out at the incorrect time and risking harm.

In the Kingdom of God, timing is a key element as well. Many people seek the will of God as to what His desire is for them, and often God will answer with a plan laid out especially for them. He is oftentimes less interested in the actions we take than their timing. He is well aware that a good step taken at the wrong time can still turn out wrong. That is why, as we travel the path of our lives, we may encounter a stoplight, put there by God Himself. It is not there to indicate that we are on the wrong path, but to regulate the timing of our journey in order to ensure safe arrival at our destination. While we as people may find the delay disheartening, the Psalmist made it clear that is part of life when he wrote "I wait for the LORD, my whole being waits, and in his word I put my hope." (Psalm 130:5) Are you sitting anxiously at a stoplight? Do you hate more than anything to wait? Be assured that the red light before you will eventually change and soon you will be making your way along life's path again.

LIFE LESSON IN THE WORD

## DAY TWENTY-ONE

# The Omnipotence Of God

Charlotte had always loved science. She liked finding order in what often appeared to be a chaotic world. She liked discovering how the universe was organized into categories, conducting experiments, and making determinations from the results. Now as a doctor, she relied on the data she received from scientific testing to determine not only what had gone wrong in the bodies of her patients, but what must be done to make it right again. But as much as Charlotte appreciated all that science could measure and understand, she knew that there were circumstances that science could not explain. She had watched patients that were not expected to make it beat the odds and pull through. She had seen people who were told that would never walk again stand to their feet and eventually learn to run. And while she had no reasonable, scientific justification for what had taken place, she understood that while scientists had worked hard to explain, predict and even control the processes of our world, there are still inexplicable events that take place outside the established norms and fly in the face of scientific laws. We call these events miracles.

As children, many of us sang that God had "the whole world in His hand." The Bible tells us that our initial evaluation was far too simple. He not only created but organizes everything in the universe and orders the heavens, the earth and beyond. From the largest planet to the smallest microbe, all things are under His scrutiny and control. Since He created all the systems and put in place all the rules that govern them, He can set those rules aside and do what we see as miraculous. Jesus said it this way, "with man this is impossible but with God, all things are possible." (Matthew 19:26) Too often, we lose sight of God's tremendous power. We begin to worship a god that is too small and weak to meet our needs. As we draw close to Him, we are quickly amazed at the awesomeness of His supremacy and might. Are you struggling to make sense of the world around you? Do you need a powerful God to do something miraculous in your life? Remember that while we as humans are confined to operate in a natural world, God operates supernaturally in the lives of His children.

LIFE LESSON IN THE WORD

DAY TWENTY-TWO

**Finishing The Task**

Cal had always been a curious boy. He had an insatiable thirst for knowledge. He especially liked to know how things worked. For a time, there was no telephone, toaster or even television that escaped his notice. He would systematically take them apart, labeling each piece and storing them carefully. After a while, his bedroom looked more like a workshop with parts of small, household appliances strewn everywhere, everything disassembled never to be reassembled. When his interest in appliances waned, he switched to building clay figures. He saw a show on television about making movies by manipulating clay figures slightly and filming each movement. When the film is shown, the inanimate objects appear to move. And while Cal started with great excitement, he soon learned that the process was much more difficult and time-consuming than he imagined and quickly moved onto his next interest. In the years that followed, he explored everything from model trains to music reproduction, each time getting half-way through, only to lose interest and move on. By the time that Cal was out of high school, he had taken over the spare room in the house, the garage and a storage shed in the back yard. Each was full from floor to ceiling with half-done projects

Like Cal, many of us have begun projects and hobbies with great excitement only to lose interest after some time. To our dismay, our lives may be littered with the residue of half-finished attempts. Some have even lost interest in their relationship with God. While we may quit on projects, God never quits on us. The Bible tells that we can be "confident of this very thing, that He who has begun a good work in you will complete it until the day of Jesus Christ." (Philippians 1:6) When we came to God, he started working on us. He began the process of healing our wounds, polishing off our rough edges, and remaking us more in His image. His goal was that we reflect His likeness to a world that desperately needs Him. No matter how long or difficult the project, God is committed to finish it and see it to its completion. Only when we see Jesus face to face will the work of God in our lives be completed. Do you feel like an unfinished work? Are you tempted to give up on God? We can take comfort in the knowledge that God will never give up on us. We must continue to seek Him and He will perfect us until we meet Him in eternity.

DAY TWENTY-THREE

## Walking With God

Hannah was never more thrilled than when saw she saw her son take his first few steps. Since walking is such an integral part of what it means to be human, it was gratifying to see her child develop; working through the intricate mechanics of balance and movement. Walking is, of course, just a controlled fall. Hannah watched as her son lifted his foot to step out, shifting his weight forward and lunging onto his front foot. He stepped tentatively, making sure that each foot hit solidly. Often his strides were unstable, and he would suddenly, and inevitably, fall. She watched nervously as he began to stare at the floor to keep track of his footing in the hopes of preventing another fall, only to trip over something in his path. What he had not yet learned was that the only way to walk with confidence is with your head held high, looking out the horizon ahead, hoping and believing that your footing is secure.

The Apostle Paul likened the journey of the Christ- follower with the act of walking. He told the church in Corinth that as believers, we must "walk by faith, not by sight." (2 Corinthians 5:7). God calls us to venture out into areas that, at first glance, seem somewhat unstable. As we follow His leading, we may find ourselves walking where our footing seems at bit wobbly and unbalanced. We may be tempted to stare at the path in the hopes of ensuring a stable footing. In doing so we take our eyes off of the One we are supposed to follow. We soon find ourselves bumping into obstacles we should have avoided. Only when we lift our eyes and fix our gaze forward, trusting in Him to lead our feet to on a sure terrain, can we successfully navigate the road God has for us. Are you walking on a steady path? Do you find yourself staring down when you should be looking up? Trust in God and He will get you to where you need to go, safe and sound.

## DAY TWENTY-FOUR

### God, Make Me Super

Kenny had always liked superheroes. As a boy, he watched his favorites on TV and read about them in comic books. He even dreamed about becoming like them, spending many a summer afternoon with a bath towel tied around his neck pretending to fly as he looked for crimes to fight and criminals to bring to justice. Among the many superheroes out there, Superman was his favorite. He liked the fact that Superman was virtually invincible. He was strong and nothing seemed to hurt him. Bullets even bounced off of his chest. But while superheroes are great, they are not completely invincible. Even as strong as he was, Superman still had his Kryptonite.

The Bible says that there will be a day that the followers of Jesus will meet him face to face. The Apostle Paul wrote that he would prefer to "be absent from the body and present with the Lord" (2 Corinthians 5:8). When we enter our heavenly home we will receive new bodies that don't wear out or age. There will be no sadness or pain or death and we will be in the presence of the Almighty, who will protect us from all harm. We will be as God intended us to be, because we will be under the watchful, caring eye of our Heavenly Father. With God on our side, we will be invincible. Are you feeling vulnerable today? Do you feel like danger and problems are lurking at your door? We can take comfort in the fact that God is watching over us, not only now, but forever. As we follow Jesus, we can look forward to the day when even the most powerful arch enemy of all will be unable to penetrate the glory of God that surrounds you. That day will be super!

# LIFE LESSON IN THE WORD

## DAY TWENTY-FIVE

## Put On A Happy Face

From the time she was little, Julia had always wanted to be an actress. It started when her parents took her to see her cousin in a high school production. The lights, the music and the interactions between the actors captivated her. When the audience laughed at a funny line, her mind raced. When the orchestra played and the characters sang, her heart soared. By the time the cast made their way on stage to take their bows at the end of the performance, she was hooked. She knew she wanted be a part of that world, so she went home and practiced. She practiced singing and dancing until her family couldn't stand it anymore. She practiced speaking and diction, learning to say each word correctly and with feeling. She even practiced facial expressions. She would sit and stare into her mirror making faces, happy faces, sad faces and the like, trying hard to capture each of a countless number of expressions. As she honed her abilities, she found something interesting. The facial muscles around her eyes and mouth that she needed to make it look as if she were crying were very similar to the muscles used to portray laughter. Though the mouth turned upward on a laugh and downward for sorrow, the facial changes and the sounds she made to portray the two different moods were nearly the same.

God has given His people a full range of emotions. We use these emotions to express our inner thoughts and feelings. And though we are complex creatures intricately designed by our Heavenly Father, our moods are as transient as the minutes of the day. There are times when the events in our lives have us thinking that we will never smile again, but we must realize those feelings will eventually fade and joy may be just around the corner. The Bible tells us that "weeping may stay for the night, but rejoicing comes in the morning." (Psalm 30:5) While there are situations that bring us pain, we must remember that they are never meant to last. They will be gone before we know it. Just as the night gives way to the morning light, so our weeping will subside, our mood will lighten and we will find ourselves rejoicing. Are your emotions on the down side? Has the play of your life turned into a tragedy? The next time you are tempted to frown remember that situations change, and God is still working in your life. You may be surprised to find that the distance between that frown and your next smile may not be as far away as you might think.

# LIFE LESSON IN THE WORD

## DAY TWENTY-SIX

### Panning For Knowledge

Shortly after Matt and Tammy got married, they moved into an old farm house on the edge of town. With the purchase of the house, they also got the 5 acres the house had rested on since 1910. While it wasn't perfect, they moved in and energetically set about making the house their home. Having been built so long ago, it had a few peculiarities that made it unique, but also challenging at times. The unusual feature that Tammy noticed first was the cabinets in the kitchen underneath the counter. Built for people of somewhat smaller stature, what the cabinets lacked in height they made up for in depth. Tammy often remarked that the cabinets were like caverns in which pots and pans could get lost and need rescuing. The pans that she used most often always seemed to be near the front, but if she needed something that she rarely used, she found herself struggling to find it. She would start by bending over to peer into the cabinet. When she still couldn't locate it, she would get down on one knee and strain to see to the back of the deep recess. If kneeling didn't allow her to see the desired pan, it was not uncommon for her to have to get down on her stomach and nearly crawl into the cabinet to retrieve it. Though being on her stomach in the middle of the kitchen floor was uncomfortable and difficult, it was only then, that her perspective allowed her to see and extract the once-lost item.

Many times, when it comes to perspective and knowledge, the Christ-follower may find themselves in the same predicament as Tammy and her lost pans. While we desire knowledge and wisdom, we often choose to look in familiar places where common information can be found. While we may find this useful in our average, daily lives, there are times when common knowledge just won't do, when simple answers will not suffice. This is when our search for wisdom requires that we put ourselves into uncomfortable and sometimes difficult positions In order to locate the knowledge, it is necessary to do what must be done. The Psalm-writer responded to God by saying, "I am your servant; give me discernment that I may understand your statutes." (Psalm 119:125) There are times that the discernment we need can only be obtained by allowing God to force us out of a place of comfort and into a place where our vantage point is changed and our position gives us unfound perspective. Are you looking for common answers to uncommon question? Are you willing to endure the uncomfortable and difficult to be able to see what you couldn't see before? Some wisdom only comes from time. Some knowledge only comes from adversity. But if we allow God to adjust our position, we will have a fresh perspective and renewed insight.

# LIFE LESSON IN THE WORD

## DAY TWENTY-SEVEN

### The Blister Principle

Penny loved getting new shoes. Her room was filled with them. The bottom of her closet, along with all the space under her bed and a large rack on her bedroom door was chocked full of shoes, in every style and color. She had shoes for every situation and outfit. Each day as she would decide what she would wear, she would always start with the shoes. While Penny loved her shoes, she found that oftentimes she developed blisters on her feet where they rubbed. The skin of the human body is especially fascinating. Soft and gentle and amazingly flexible, it can become irritated when chafed against something solid. The skin, in response to such abuse, puffs up in a blister, so as to provide some protection from the injured area. If treated properly, the skin will respond and the injury will eventually heal. But if ignored, and the overuse continues, the blister will soon develop into a callus, a thick, hard, piece of skin. The callus is another way the skin protects itself from injury, leaving a toughened spot that is hard on the outside and with little to no feeling on the inside.

Many Christ-followers understand the difficulties endured by the skin. We often come in contact with a world full of difficult and hurting people, leaving the tender-hearted Christian feeling offended or abused. The natural response to such an offense of the heart is a puffy blister designed for protection. If the offense is treated properly, the heart will be repaired and soon return to normal function. If left untreated, the offended heart will soon callus, leading to hardness and an inability to respond to the feelings of others. The Bible reminds us that we must then make sure to keep our hearts free from such hardness when it tells us to "get rid of all bitterness, rage and anger, brawling and slander, along with every form of malice. Be kind and compassionate to one another, forgiving each other, just as in Christ God forgave you." (Ephesians 4:31-32) Have been hurt by others? Have calluses somehow developed on your heart? Be sure to check your heart daily for signs of painful blistering and treat anything you find accordingly, because God wants his people to always be tenderhearted.

## DAY TWENTY-EIGHT

### The Undo Button

Having never worked with computers before, Cathy was more than just a little intimidated by them. Though she had watched her grandchildren maneuver the mouse around the screen, clicking on things and moving them with the greatest of ease, she was sure that if she tried to do the same thing she would somehow break something, leaving the expensive device worthless. Her son had tried to teach her what to do, but her lingering fear made her hesitant. Then one day as she was sitting at the table reading the newspaper and her grandson sat next to her working on his laptop for a school project, she heard him remark in disgust. He typed something wrong. As Cathy watched, he moved his mouse up to an icon and the mistake suddenly disappeared. Astonished, she asked him what he had done. With a smirk he said, "That's the undo button Grandma. Whatever you've done can be undone with a click of the mouse." From then on, Cathy conquered her fear of computers. She learned how to operate each program and became not only proficient but productive in her efforts.

When God created the world, he knew that his children would eventually make a mistake. He knew that as they went about their day, someone somewhere would make a wrong choice or go in a direction that was contrary to his word. He knew that their actions would prove both hurtful and harmful. Knowing all of this, God made an "Undo" button for us. The Bible tells us that "If we confess our sins, He is faithful and just and will forgive us our sins and purify us from all unrighteousness." (1 John 1:9) His word tells us that if we go to God and admit that we have made a mistake, He will click His "Undo" button and it will be as if we had never done anything wrong. The page that was full of errors will be wiped as clean as it was before. Have you made an error today? Would you like to go back and do it over? Go to God and acknowledge your mistake and He will make it right. Then you can go forward with your life and be productive.

## DAY TWENTY-NINE

## Finding The Right Solution

Jennifer had a serious problem. It seemed she had mice in her house. She noticed them one day when she opened her cupboard and discovered one gnawing on bag of rice, while several others ran across her floor. Disgusted and perplexed as to what to do, she purchased several cats to chase away the mice. Before long the mice were gone, but the cats just sat around her house leaving fur balls everywhere. They sharpened their claws on her furniture and climbed up her drapes. Unhappy with living with a house full of cats, she got some dogs to chase away the cats, and soon her house was completely cat-free. In no time at all, the dogs chewed up all her shoes and made messes all over her carpet. Being miserable in a house full of dogs, she got a lion to chase away the dogs. In a very short time, there was not a dog to be found in her house. Then to her amazement, she realized that it was not safe to live in a house with a lion, so she was quickly forced to move. After getting settled in her new house, everything was fine, until one day she noticed saw a small brown mouse running across her living room floor.

Much like Jennifer, we are faced with obstacles and dilemmas in life. Oftentimes, we are tempted to use earthly methods and means to bring about solutions. We do our best, only to find that our solutions have created greater problems, leaving us worse off than we were before. While we stand in front of the mess we've made and scratch our head, contemplating our next move, we must come to realize that God has means at his disposal to solve all the problems we face if we will only listen and do as He says. David, the psalm-writer expressed it this way. "How precious to me are your thoughts, God! How vast is the sum of them!" (Psalm 139:17) Do you develop seemingly fool-proof plans that only seem to backfire? Have you tried to solve your problems only to make things worse? Ask God's help in solving the problem and soon you will be amazed at how good your life will be.

## DAY THIRTY

## **Give Me A Brick**

As Owen left his brother Max's house, he swore he would never set foot in it again. The two men were at odds over the three hundred acres of land their recently deceased father had left them. In his will, their father had given his sons the land to share but they couldn't seem to agree as to what should be done with it. Max wanted to continue farming the land like this father and grandfather had done, while Owen wanted to sell it to developers for a hefty profit. The brothers decided that the only way to resolve the dispute was to divide the property evenly. They agreed that the dividing line would be a creek which ran through the property. As Owen went out to look at his side of the property, he determined that few people would want to live and shop right next to a working farm so he hired a brick mason to build a wall that would separate his property from his brother's. Owen instructed the mason that the bricks would be delivered to the site and a wall was to be built so that Max's farm was obstructed from view. Two weeks later, the mason contacted Owen telling him the work had been completed. A bit surprised, Owen drove to site only to realize that instead of building a wall, the mason had built a large ornate bridge over the creek, joining the two properties. In that moment, Owen realized he had been wrong. Family was more important than personal gain. He decided then and there to reconcile with his brother and make things right.

As Christ-followers, we are family. And just like any family there are bound to be disagreements and squabbles. It is not the fact that disputes happen but how we handle them that sets us apart. The Bible tells us that we are to "bear with each other and forgive whatever grievances you may have against one another." (Colossians 3:13) Just like any parent, God wants his children to love one another and never let petty bickering and personal disputes come between them. We must remember that though we may not always agree, we represent God to a world looking for cooperation instead of strife. If we can learn to put aside our differences for the greater good of the kingdom of God, we send a powerful message as to what the healing power of God is all about. Have old grievances separated you from the family you should love? Is it time to let go of the past? Each day God gives us a brick. We decide what we do with it. We can choose to build bridges or choose to build walls.

## DAY THIRTY-ONE

## The Omnipresence Of God

Holly watched with great interest as Professor Samuels brought an empty jar into the classroom and placed it on the table in the front of the room. He asked his students, "Is the jar full?" The students confidently replied "No" The professor then pulled out a bag of rocks and gravel and poured them into the jar until no more gravel would fit. He asked his students again, "Is the jar full?" Some said yes while other others disagreed. He told them that as long as there were space left in the jar between the stones that the jar was still not full. He then took out some sand and poured it in the jar and filled up the spaces between the rocks. He again asked his students, "Is the jar full?" More students were sure that the jar was full. But the professor again told them that there were still empty spaces to be filled. He pulled out a pitcher of water and poured it into the jar until it overran the sides. "Now", he told the students, "there is no more empty space in the jar. It is finally full."

Just like the water, God is able to come and fill in the cracks and crevices of our lives. There is no place that is too big or too small for Him to occupy; no area He cannot inhabit. The Bible tells us that He is everywhere at all times. "The LORD himself goes before you and will be with you; he will never leave you nor forsake you." (Deuteronomy 31:8) No matter where we are or what we encounter, God is there with us every step of the way. When Moses was called to take a message back to the children of Israel, he asked God to tell him who was sending him. God said His name was "I AM." He is not the God of yesterday, or tomorrow. He is the God of today, right now, wherever we are and He remains with us forever. Does it seem like everyone has left you? Are you feeling alone? The One who is everywhere, at all times, wants you to know that He is with you now and will be with you until the end.

## DAY THIRTY-TWO

## Resistance Is Not Futile

Wade had always been a fan of drive-in movies. He remembered going with his parents as a kid, playing on the playground until the move started and watching the cheesy movies until he fell asleep. These less-than-cinematic classics often focused on unheard of scenarios where escaped mutant animals transformed by exposure to atomic rays wreaked havoc on major metropolitan areas, or outlaw biker gangs took over whole towns. But one of the most revisited themes of the drive-in era was the story of invading space aliens. Over and over the public was besieged by tales of little green men in space ships coming to earth from some other planet to take over our world. The superior technology of these extraterrestrial aggressors made our earthly weapons useless and we were defenseless as they set about their plans to enslave the earth. Often the leader of the alien horde explained their plans in great detail, letting his earthling servants know that, "Resistance is futile". Though some might worry, Wade knew that every one of these stories ended with the earthlings ultimately defeating their alien captors and peace and order would eventually being returned to the earth.

While we as followers of Jesus may see those old movies and smile at the silliness of the situations portrayed there, we must be aware that we face a real enemy that would like nothing more than to take over the whole world and enslave the human race. The Bible tells us that the enemy of our souls is a "roaring lion looking for someone to devour" (1 Peter 5:8), and that he has come "to steal and kill and destroy." (John 10:10) While these words may fill us with fear and lead us to believe that, like earthlings facing the alien invasion, "resistance is futile", nothing could be further from the truth. God's word assures us all to defeat this formidable foe all we must do is "Submit yourself to God. Resist the devil and he will flee from you." (James 4:7) The formula is that simple. While we alone are no match for the devil and his forces on our own, if we will only submit ourselves to an All-Powerful God and resist the forces of the evil one, the end of our story will be the same as the drive-in movie. Are you afraid of the devil and his evil schemes? Do you feel powerless to foil his plans? As we submit ourselves to God, we can acquire the necessary power to defeat an alien invader and allow peace and order to once again return to our world.

# LIFE LESSON IN THE WORD

## DAY THIRTY-THREE

### Forgetting Who I'm Talking To

Janet was hired as a temp by a large accounting firm. Even though she was just out of business school and working her first job, she had big dreams of what she would do, and where in the company she would end up. She saw herself running one of the departments, managing staff, heading up meetings, and making decisions that would affect the company's bottom line. However today, she was a temp; assigned to answer the phones for a vice president. One day as she was transferring some files to another floor, an older man in a blue business suit got on the elevator with her. To break the awkward silence, the older man inquired who she was and what she did. Janet explained her situation and her dreams of doing great things given the opportunity. The old man then asked what she would change if she had the power. Without thinking, Janet began to tell the older man what was wrong with the company. She complained about the management and ownership of the firm, explaining it was antiquated and out of touch and something needed to be done. Just then, the elevator doors opened and the older man smiled as he stepped out of the elevator. As the elevator doors closed, Janet looked up to see a picture of that same older man surrounded by a group of people. She realized, to her surprise, that she had been talking to the president of the company.

Job encountered a situation similar to Janet's. He was enduring difficulty and began to complain to God about his circumstances. What he failed to realize was, he had directed his objections to the One that holds the universe and everything in it in the palm of His hand. He didn't realize who he was talking to. After listening to Job's list of grievances, God intervened with a question. "Where were you when I laid the earth's foundation? Tell me, if you understand. Who marked off its dimensions? Surely you know! Who stretched a measuring line across it?" (Job 38:4-5) Over the next two chapters, God asked Job a series of questions that no human being could ever fully understand, much less answer. God showed a man, who was fixated on his particular circumstances, the enormity of the cosmos. In a second, Job's problems seemed insignificant by comparison.

Are you tempted to complain to God about your circumstances? Do you tell Him what is wrong instead of following His leading? Though we go through trials, God knows what we can handle. We can rest assured that He has everything under control and if we will simply follow Him, He will lead us to our ultimate good.

## DAY THIRTY-FOUR

### What Me Worry?

Angela was a self-proclaimed worry wart. She worried about everything. When she was little, she worried about her grades in school and whether the other kids liked her. She worried about her parents and the health of her cat. Now, as a wife and mother, she worried about her kids, how they were doing in school and how they would turn out. She worried about her husband as he traveled for work. Would he be OK? Her imagination conjured horrible scenarios that always ended in tragedy and despair. She didn't like to worry, and while she knew that worrying never actually solved anything and nothing she ever worried about ever came true, she just couldn't help herself. She felt helpless in a scary world where danger lurked around every corner. Though she tried to comfort herself, thinking that worrying kept her sharp and focused, all it ever made her was anxious and uneasy, keeping her emotions tied up and her nerves on edge.

Many of God's people are like Angela. They feel like they must examine every scenario. Often, they live in fear that difficulties will catch up to them and swallow them whole. While God has not called us to live carelessly, He has not called us to live in the oppression of worry as well. Worry is nothing more than fear that has been well thought out. It is a reaction to the helplessness and uncertainty of what the future might hold. But Jesus said, "Do not worry about tomorrow, for tomorrow will worry about itself." (Matthew 6:34) He counsels His followers not to be so distracted with the awful events that could happen tomorrow that they miss the actual events that are taking place right in front of them. While none of us knows what tomorrow holds, He reassures us that nothing that will confront us that He is not able to lead us through. Are you worried for nothing? Are you spending today fretting tomorrows? Place your trust in the One who has committed Himself to guide us not only through today, but tomorrow and the rest of eternity.

## DAY THIRTY-FIVE

### Following Through

Violet was very particular when it came to paying bills. She never liked to owe anyone anything. So, she was rather annoyed when she noticed that her electric bill had a balance from the previous month. With hesitation, she feverishly began checking her records; sure that she had paid it. She found a copy of the check she had written and the update in the checking account record. Determined she was right, she went over to the phone on her desk to call the company and complain. As she picked up the phone she noticed the sealed envelope with a stamp on it hiding in a stack of bills yet to be paid. She didn't know whether to laugh or cry. Though she had done everything necessary to pay the bill, she forgot the last important step. She forgot to put it in the mail. Her failure to follow through on that one missed step negated all the work she had done up to then.

Coaches often tell their players that it's not how they begin that marks their success or failure, it is how they finish. The same is true in the life of the disciples of Christ. Jesus advised the churches in Revelation that a reward is prepared for "the one who is victorious and does my will to the end." (Revelation 2:26) Whether it's paying bills or following Jesus, it does us no good to be involved if we fail to follow through to the finish. Like Violet, we get no credit for going halfway or even most of the way. We will only receive God's best if we pursue Him all the way to the end. Did you start out well only to get lost in the middle? Have you missed a step along the way? Commit yourself to follow God all the way to the finish. You'll find a great reward in the end.

## DAY THIRTY-SIX

## Jump Starting Gospel

Though Monday morning came every week, Andy had never been ready for it. This Monday morning, he was even less ready than usual. Having forgotten to reset his alarm, he had overslept and was running very late. As he rushed to his car to start his daily commute, he turned the key but nothing happened. Feeling helpless and a little embarrassed, Andy quickly realized the battery in his car was dead. With no way to get his car started, he called his friend Ray to come over and give him a jumpstart. Anyone who has driven a car for very long knows that jumpstarting a car is a simple process. It requires attaching the dead, lifeless battery to one that is working and full of life. As the batteries are connected, power is drawn from the healthy battery to the one in need of energy. As soon as Ray finished hooking up the battery, Andy's car sprang to life and he was on his way.

We, as believers in Jesus, are called to jump start the world around us. Jesus told his disciples to remain in Jerusalem to "receive power" so they might become his witnesses. (Acts 1:8) When we draw close to Jesus, we are filled with His power. We are filled to capacity like the charge in a healthy battery. As we draw close to others, the power flows through us so that we can recharge those around us whose batteries have lost power and become lifeless. The power is released and those that were dull and motionless spring to life again with renewed vigor. Are you full of the power only God can provide? Or are you working at half wattage? Connect yourself to the Source of all power and let Him charge you up so that you can provide renewed life and strength to those in need.

## DAY THIRTY-SEVEN

## Licking Life's Tigers

Grace liked it when her mother read to her, especially when it was from Dr Seuss. Her favorite was a story called, "I Can Lick 30 Tigers Today". It is about a young man who wakes up in the morning feeling nearly invincible. He greets the day with a smile on his face and a positive disposition as he looks forward to what wonderful things await him. His optimistic outlook leads him to believe that he can do anything, including licking 30 tigers. He emerges from his house confident in his abilities and ready to meet the day, until he comes face to face with the 30 tigers he spoke of earlier. Now confronted with the frightening and overwhelming challenge that 30 tigers would bring about, he begins to make excuses as to why 30 may be too large a number. As the book continues, he systematically finds a series of questionable reasons for whittling down the number of tigers and sending them on their way. Finally, as the book ends, he is faced with only 1 tiger left, and with all his excuses gone, he simply explains that it is too late in the day to take on a tiger, and his ordeal is over.

Often times, as disciples of Jesus, we may immerge from our prayer time or a particularly meaningful church service and, being full of faith, believing that we have what it takes to conquer the world around us. We optimistically believe that we can single-handedly defeat the enemy of our soul and bring his kingdom to an end. We believe this until we are actually embroiled in the battle that such a victory would entail. Then, in the midst of difficulty, our optimism quickly fades and we begin to search for excuses that will provide us with a way of escape. But we have something that the boy in the Dr Seuss story did not have. We have the power of God on our side. In his letter to the church in Philippi, the Apostle Paul encouraged them by letting them know that we as believers "can do all things through Christ who strengthens" (Philippians 4:13) Have you felt up-beat only to face adversity that looks to beat you down? Did you step out only to get stepped on? God is not offended by our optimism but desires that we put our hope not in our ability, but His. When we do, we can confidently and triumphantly overcome whatever comes our way.

## DAY THIRTY-EIGHT

## The Omniscience Of God

Hunter sat down at his computer to start his geography project. To get a good grade, his teacher had insisted that the students not only research the major cities of a chosen country from around the world, but plan a trip that would encompass those cities. Now faced with the awesome task of not only finding information about historic sites and tourist attractions, he also had to determine the cost of the restaurants, hotels and transportation on this fictitious vacation. While not long ago this information would have been almost impossible to find and compile, with the use of the internet, almost all knowledge is available at the click of a mouse, no matter how odd or obscure. Within minutes, Hunter was able to ask questions and get answers to all kinds of complex situations and scenarios. With the help of his computer, he simply tapped into the collective knowledge of people from all over the world. Despite the boom of knowledge we have gained, we as people are still faced with problems for which we have no solution and questions for which we have no answer. Though much more information is available to us than ever before in human history, there are times we must humbly say "I don't know."

Though human knowledge is finite, the God that we serve has no such problem with a lack of knowledge. His omniscience is complete. He knows everything about everything that has taken place or will ever take place everywhere in the universe. He is never surprised or taken aback by the things that transpire in our lives, because He knows everything there is to know about us as well. He knew us long before we were born. He saw us, even at the foundations of the world. If all of the collective knowledge of all the people who have ever lived on this planet, from ages past until now, were assembled together and piled up, it would fill a thimble compared to the ocean of God's knowledge and understanding. The Psalm-writer explained it this way "Great is our Lord and mighty in power; his understanding has no limit." (Psalm 147:5) Atop all of that knowledge and understanding, lives a God who loves us and wants to be with us. Are you overwhelmed with the things you don't know or understand? Do you feel particularly uninformed these days?

Remember that the One who knows you best and knows everything about you, loves you more than you can ever understand and wants to share His love with you.

## DAY THIRTY-NINE

## Keep You Eye On The Ball

As a young child playing catch with his dad in the backyard, Phillip was given the age-old advice "Keep your eye on the ball." The key to success in any sport is focus. Phillip found out quickly that problems arise when a player diverts their attention from the ball, even if only for a split second. We can have success in the palm of our hand, only to miss it as we look away at something else. Focus is essential for success in life as well. What we look at, what we decide to focus on, will affect our actions, which will ultimately affect the outcome in which we find ourselves. Those whose concentration is diverted, whose attention is fragmented will find it nearly impossible to achieve their ultimate goal. But when we focus our eyes on the prize, we take the first step to winning

Focus is a fundamental part of the life of the followers of Jesus as well. What we continue to look intently upon will determine our success or failure in our life with Christ. Scripture tells us, as believers, to "fix our eyes on Jesus." (Hebrews 12:2) We must affix our gaze and maintain our attention on him and he will lead us along the correct paths of our life. The Apostle Peter learned this lesson one day in the middle of a rough sea. When he looked at Jesus, he could do the impossible, but as soon as his attention was averted elsewhere, he began to sink. God has called us to do the impossible as well. Only when we determine to keep our eyes on Jesus will the things that are outside our scope come into focus. Are you distracted by many things? Do you find your attention being diverted from the one thing that is most important? Take time today to focus on Jesus and you will take the next step on the road to success.

## DAY FORTY

## Vital Signs

Tina was, by all measures, a workaholic. It seemed that every waking moment of her life was filled with some activity. She was so busy that her friends referred to her as "The Bumble Bee", always buzzing from one thing to another. It was in the midst of one of her busy days that Tina began to feel strange. She noticed that her heart seemed to be racing and she was beginning to sweat. Soon, she felt light-headed and a sharp pain penetrated the middle of her chest. Convinced she was having a heart attack, she called for paramedics who arrived quickly. They found her on the couch in her apartment, conscious but confused. They took her blood pressure and monitored her breathing as they transported her to the hospital. Once there, doctors did an EKG to check her heart. But the longer she was there, the more she was convinced it was not a heart problem, but possibly a panic attack brought on by stress. The doctors evaluated all the tests they had performed and soon confirmed Tina's diagnosis. What had originally felt like an emergency soon changed to something less severe. The vital signs taken on the outside of her body had confirmed what was really going on inside of her.

Something similar takes place in the life of the Christ-follower. God works on the inside of us, but for it to do any good, it must make its way outside. The Bible tells us that "in him we live and move and have our being." (Acts 17:28) As we get into God and He gets into us, changes happen on the inside of us. We experience life like we have never known before. We enjoy the freedom of movement where we were once bound and we are given the ability to take pleasure in our daily lives, letting go of our past and being assured of our future. Our vital signs indicate that something new is taking place and those around us soon begin to notice changes in us; changes that radiate to the outside from what is happening on the inside. What are your vital signs saying about you? Does your outside reflect the work of God going on inside of you? Start today to allow God to work on the inside of you and before long the good that is happening on the inside will shine through to all those around you.

## DAY FORTY-ONE

## A Great Day Coming

Jerry had been pastor of his church for some time when one day he told his congregation, "Your best days are ahead of you!" Many people in the church were surprised by a statement like that. There had been many great days in the history of their church. They had seen God do tremendous things as He moved in the lives of people. Many wondered how it could get any better than that. As we get older, it is not uncommon to look back with tremendous affection on the great days of our past. We remember the wonderful experiences that serve as the landmarks of our lives. We may remember high school graduation, our wedding day, buying our first house or the birth of children. There are countless personal milestones of accomplishment or recognition, and times of great fondness. Some have seen these great milestones come and go. Once those days are behind us, to what do we have to look forward? After living a life full of wonder and splendor, how can we look to the future and believe that better days are ahead of us?

For disciples of Jesus, there is a day coming which outshines all the wonderful days of our lives combined. There will be a day when we will pass from this life to the life to come. We will move from a world of pain and sorrow, a world of hunger and want, a world where both tremendous good and unspeakable evil can be seen, to a world where God rules and reigns. On that day, we will enter the holy city and stand before God as Jesus greets us saying, "'Come, you who are blessed by my Father; take your inheritance, the kingdom prepared for you since the creation of the world." (Matthew 25:34) All of the best days of this life, if they were stacked one upon another, could not compare to that day. Have you had good times in your past? Do you wonder if you will ever see good times like those again? Keep your eyes on Jesus and you can walk with confidence knowing you have a bright future ahead and your best days are still to come.

# LIFE LESSON IN THE WORD

## DAY FORTY-TWO

### Is That Really Me?

When Paige turned on her computer and logged into Facebook, she couldn't believe her eyes. Her friends had taken her out for her birthday the week before and now the pictures they had taken were all over her page. Though they had not done anything immoral or embarrassing, she couldn't help but cringe when she viewed each snapshot. As she honestly looked at herself, she was shocked at her appearance. The person in those pictures looked older and more out of shape than she thought she was. The gray hair that she was convinced was unnoticeable, that she thought was somewhat hidden, was fully on display. Her clothes seemed frumpy and out of date. While she thought she was fooling everyone else, the only person she was fooling was herself. With a class reunion coming up in a few months, she determined she needed a change. A new hair style, some new outfits and weight-loss program were in store. The next day, she downloaded a meal plan from an online diet, signed up at a local gym and started shopping for a new look. By the time the reunion arrived, she walked in looking great. As she posed for pictures with her former classmates, she couldn't wait for the whole world to see. Who would have thought that honestly looking at one snapshot could have had such an effect?

Oftentimes, as followers of Christ, we find ourselves in a situation similar to Paige. We think we're doing just fine in our relationship with God, and though we know we're not perfect, we don't sense any urgency to modify our approach or make changes in order to be the best we can be. The Bible tells us that "Anyone who listens to the word but does not do what it says is like someone who looks at his face in a mirror and, after looking at himself, goes away and immediately forgets what he looks like." (James 1:23-24) As we read the Bible, we are often confronted with the truth of God. In a moment, our wrong actions and attitudes are exposed to us and we cringe. It is at that point that we must decide whether to deal with the unsightliness of our condition and do what it takes to make it better, or perpetually deceive ourselves into believing that everything is alright. We must make hard choices about our present and our future. Have you been confronted with the truth of God's word? Or has contentedness in your current situation lead to complacency? The Bible is a mirror to our soul. If we don't like what we see, we must decide to change the image or ignore the reflection. Our decision will determine our success or failure not only in this life, but in the life to come.

# LIFE LESSON IN THE WORD

## DAY FORTY-THREE

### Speak For Me

Austin had had a crush on Amber for as long as he could remember. They had gone to grade school, middle school and high school together, and now as students at the local community college, Austin saw her almost every day. He went out of his way to "accidently" run into her. While he wanted more than anything to talk to her, he just couldn't. Though he was smart and athletic and some might say even handsome, he was very shy around girls. He knew that Amber was popular and very attractive. The very thought of talking to her left him speechless. He had envisioned several times what would happen if he approached her to express his feelings. He would get nervous and tongue-tied and say the wrong thing. He would blow his one chance with Amber and everyone around would just laugh. He couldn't stand that kind of rejection. Finally, in desperation, he asked his friend Jack to intercede for him and speak to her on his behalf. Austin watched as Jack talked to her and she smiled as she looked over at Austin. It seems that Amber had always really liked Austin as well. She was shy and was waiting for him to make the first move. Thanks to Jack's help, they are a happy couple, building a relationship and enjoying each other as they grow closer together.

Many people in our world today have questions about God. They long for love and acceptance. They desire to be near a God who loves and understands them, but many see God as too big and unapproachable to be bothered with the affairs of common people. They imagine coming close to him in his vast power and awesome glory and envision disastrous results. They may want to reach out to God but are unsure of what to say or how to start. For them, there is hope. The Bible says that Jesus "lives to intercede" to God for us. (Hebrews 7:25) He speaks to God on our behalf and serves as a go-between for us so that we can develop a personal, intimate relationship with God. He who was once human, has bridged the gap and made it possible for us to have the relationship with God that we have always wanted. Are you intimidated by trying to reach out to a God you see as aloof? Do you hold back when you want to draw close? Remember that Jesus, our trusted friend, has paved the way for us to draw near to God and begin a life-fulfilling relationship with the One we have been longing for.

# LIFE LESSON IN THE WORD

## DAY FORTY-FOUR

## Doing The Hokey Pokey

Bruno was new to this country. As an immigrant from Poland, he was unfamiliar with many of the customs of his new American friends. So when he was invited to the wedding of the daughter of one of his co-workers, he was unsure of what to expect. While he thought the ceremony was very nice, he found the wedding reception very peculiar. After a nice meal and some pleasant conversation, all in attendance were invited to dance. Just as things got going and the dance floor was full, the deejay began to play the Hokey Pokey. Like a wave of humanity, everyone clapped and gathered into a big circle. Bruno was swept up in the wave and before he knew it he was putting his right arm in then taking it back out. As the game progressed, he had inserted and retrieved every significant body part until the song told him to put his whole self in. Looking around the room, he noticed everyone jumping forward then back. While he never did understand what was to be accomplished in this song, his friends assured him that that was really what it all was all about.

Many Christ-followers treat their relationship with God like the hokey pokey. One day, they invest part of themselves into God's kingdom only later to pull back out. While they may enjoy dancing with God, they never will find true contentment in Him. What many fail to realize is that God does not want a part of us for a short period of time. He wants us to put our whole self into his kingdom and leave it there. Only then will we experience the love, joy, and peace God has in store for us. The Apostle Paul made this clear in his letter to the church in Corinth when he said "whoever sows sparingly will also reap sparingly, and whoever sows generously will also reap generously." (2 Corinthians 9:6) Are you fully invested in God's kingdom? Are you in one day and out the next? Until we invest ourselves completely into a relationship with God we will never experience the full benefits that God has to offer. While others enjoy His presence, we will never really know what He is all about.

## DAY FORTY-FIVE

## Missing Labels

While she was growing up, Tina's father was the manager of a grocery store. As a perk for his job, her father got to bring home food that was damaged while in transit to his store. Torn cereal boxes and dented soda cans lined the shelves of the family's pantry. But the most interesting items on the shelves were the cans of food whose labels had been torn off during shipping. Each night, Tina's mother would open a can never knowing what was in it. It could be anything from tomatoes to peaches, from fruit cocktail to artichokes. From the contents of these unmarked cans, she would build the family's evening meal. So each night, it was a mystery as to what was for dinner; the family never knowing what surprise lay inside the unlabeled cans.

While labels used to distinguish food cans can prove helpful, labels placed on people can be hurtful and destructive. Too often, people label others who are different from themselves based upon race, economics, or church denomination. Although labels on food cans can accurately explain what's inside, labels on people only serve to divide us from each other and can never truly describe the content of a person or their character. The Apostle Paul reminded the church in Galatia of this when he wrote, "There is neither Jew nor Greek, slave nor free, male nor female, for you are all one in Christ Jesus." (Galatians 3:28) Are you quick to slap a label on someone who is different? Do you struggle to define the content of person based upon what is on the outside? Begin today to look past the differences we find in each other to see the true nature of those around you and you just may find an exciting and welcome surprise in an unlabeled can.

## DAY FORTY-SIX

## Choose Wisely

Marlene was overwhelmed by the choices that lay before her. Every day it seemed that there was an endless list of decisions that had to be made. Baskin Robbins advertised 31 flavors, one for every day of the month. Blockbuster, Netflix and Red Box have over a million titles from which to choose. McDonald's, whose original menu only contained 7 items, had changed over the years to provide consumers with a cornucopia of fast food delights. She even found a simple trip to the grocery store for the staples had turned into a never-ending list of options as to the size and type of milk, bread, eggs and butter she would buy. Economists tell us that we are confronted with limited resources of time, talent and treasure and yet before us lay endless array of choices. Never in the course of human history has this been truer than now. Given the countless number of choices that are available to us, the task then is not just to choose, but to choose wisely.

The children of Israel were faced with some of the same challenges of choice that we face in modern America. Around them lived people who worshipped all kinds of gods. After having left Egypt and as they were about to enter the Promised Land, Joshua challenged the Israelites to "choose for yourselves this day whom you will serve" (Joshua 24:15) Notice the question is not a matter of if we will serve, but which god or entity it will be. We as people, as a matter of course, will pledge our service and loyalty to someone or something. That is not up for debate. The good news is that we get to choose. Given the dizzying array of options, the task then is not just to choose but to choose wisely. Joshua punctuates the conversation on choices by announcing his, "But as for me and my household, we will serve the LORD." Are you plagued by uncertainty? Do you find yourself distracted by all the choices that vie for your attention? When we stand at the crossroad of decision, it is essential that we take the time to survey our options and wisely choose the path that leads us to God.

## DAY FORTY-SEVEN

## A Funny Thing Happened

Lee had always been considered a funny guy by the people who knew him. He had been told more than once that he should try out as a stand-up comedian. Many thought he had what it took to do very well in comedy. Lee had just one problem. He was afraid. He was uncertain that the jokes he made up as he drove to work each day were funny. He doubted that the talent he had was enough to entertain people and make them laugh. His biggest fear was not what would happen if people laughed, it was what would happen if they didn't. Comedians call it bombing. It is when their best material falls flat in front of an audience that doesn't find it funny. Lee knew that if he got up on stage, sooner or later he would bomb and the fear of that kept him from ever trying. So it went this way for Lee for many years. He was the funniest guy at the workplace but it never went any farther than that. Until one day, when he came into work, he found a flier on his desk about an open audition for amateur comedians to display their talent for a local show. All the guys at the office dared Lee to perform. With the backing of his friends, Lee took the risk and performed in the show. As he heard the laughter of the people his heart soared, knowing that not only had he done well, but he had faced his fear and won.

Many who wish to pursue a life with God can identify with Lee. They want to move forward but are hampered by fear and doubt that keeps them sidelined. Though they want to be bold and do great things for God, they are concerned about the consequences of what it will mean. They wonder whether they have what it takes to be used by God to affect change in the world in which they live. But we cannot afford to be timid or fearful. God has called his children to impact this world for him and make a difference for good. The Bible tells that "the Spirit God gave us does not make us timid, but gives us power, love and self-discipline." (2 Timothy 1:7) While stepping out in faith may seem risky, with the backing of the Spirit of God, even if we face a hostile audience, we will ultimately prevail. Has fear kept you from stepping out in faith with God? Have the risks of being all that God wants prevented you from even trying? Decide today to put fear in its place. While with any new adventure there are always risks, we can face them in confidence knowing that God will prepare us and provide for us as we pursue His will for our lives.

## DAY FORTY-EIGHT

## **The Breakdown**

Jeremy was having a very bad day. It started when he was late for the early morning meeting. As he crept through bumper to bumper traffic, he tried to call ahead to let them know where he was, only to find that his cell phone had died. Though he looked for the charger he kept in his car, all he found in the compartment between the seats was a CD and some candy wrappers left over from his daughter who had driven his car the night before. When he finally got to the meeting, he set up his laptop and projector only to find that his computer couldn't locate internet service and the bulb on the projector was burned out. In this world of faster and better electronic devices, it is not uncommon that people who use them become dependent on them. It can be mind-boggling and heartbreaking when the technology we count on doesn't work. The look of surprise and dismay that comes across the face of someone who realizes that their cell phone has lost its power or their computer program has somehow gone haywire is astounding. In a world where nothing is perfect, where things get old and wear out, where some of our best laid plans fall flat, it should not shock us at all.

For those who follow Jesus, living on this earth will mean that disappointment and distress will, at times, be a part of our lives. While God forgives our sins and puts us on a path to righteousness and eternal life, some have been lead to believe that living a Godly life is a mystical cure for any and all negative situations they might encounter. Yet the Bible tells us that God "causes his sun to rise on the evil and the good, and sends rain on the righteous and the unrighteous." (Matthew 5:45) Though we are God's children, we are not immune to the problems and struggles that permeate this world. The good news is that even though we may find ourselves in difficulty as we walk through this life, God gives us the ability to rise above our circumstances and rejoice in the midst of it all. We can have peace and joy even when things around us go wrong and people let us down. Are you dealing with difficulties? Do you feel betrayed by God? We must understand that the path of righteousness is not a bypass around life's problems, but an expressway through them to a bright and blessed future on the other side.

## DAY FORTY-NINE

## **A View From The Top**

As Daphne flew in a plane for the first time, she was shocked to realize how much different the world looks from the air than it does on the ground. Seeing the world from that angle gave her a fresh perspective on the things that we see each day. Buildings, vehicles, roads and fields, which loom large from a horizontal viewpoint seemed almost microscopic from the air. From a vertical vantage point, vehicles traveling down a road look like ants following each other in column formation down a tiny dirt path. Fields which seem to go on for miles here on earth, from the air, look like a patchwork quilt laid out in various shapes and sizes. Once she saw the world from above, she never looked at the earth the same way again. Her perspective once she came back down was changed forever, because the way a person sees things, their perspective, is key how successful they will be as they move through life.

While we, as people, see our lives from the horizontal view, God sees us from a different perspective. From His vertical vantage point, the obstacles that loom so large to us appear as nothing to Him. He tells us in scripture that "as the heavens are higher than the earth, so are my ways are higher than your ways and my thoughts than your thoughts." (Isaiah 55:9) He doesn't see things from a horizontal human perspective. His view is vertical, looking down from the heavens, so that the things that appear large to us look microscopic in His view. What's even more exciting is that He invites us to look at life from his point of view, giving us a fresh perspective on the world around us. Do the obstacles in your path seem large and overwhelming? Do you need a fresh perspective on what is in front of you? Take a look at life from God's perspective. It will change the way you see the world and your place in it.

## DAY FIFTY

## God & The Microwave

Tom didn't know much about cooking. His wife normally handled that. With her away visiting her mother and two kids to feed, Tom felt somewhat at ease because he did know how to use a microwave oven. Since its inception in the early seventies, the microwave has revolutionized cooking in this country. What used to take several minutes or even hours, now takes only a few seconds. The microwave has changed it all. As Tom stood there watching through the little window as his dinner spun slowly inside, he was struck with the idea that though he could use a microwave rather effectively, he had no clue how a microwave actually worked. Not only did he not understand how the microwave does what it does, he had little desire to learn. He believed that the science was beyond his understanding. So when the makers of the microwave told him not to use metal in the machine or that eggs were dangerous to heat up, he didn't question them. He accepted their admonition in faith, believing that they knew best. While he still didn't fully understand how the microwave worked, he still went on using it every day, not knowing what he would do without it.

God is very similar to the microwave. Someone once said that "God works in mysterious ways.", and to us this may be true. Because we as people cannot figure out how or why God works, many have decided not to follow Him. Some have determined that He is unfair, cruel or even evil because they could not fathom his rationale for allowing certain circumstances to occur. But just because we cannot understand God and His ways, does not mean that we cannot love Him and follow Him. He has given us His word to study in order to begin to get to know His character. Though it will not allow us to fully understand God, because no human could, it gives us insight into who He is and how He operates, thus allowing us to understand that He knows best. The psalmist writes "I run in the path of your commands, for you have broadened my understanding." (Psalm 119:32) Are you confused by the workings of God? Do His ways baffle you? Don't let that discourage you from following him.

Keep seeking Him every day and before long, you won't know what you did without Him.

LIFE LESSON IN THE WORD

DAY FIFTY-ONE

## The Great Exchange

Leslie was as surprised as anyone when she received the letter from a lawyer's office. It seems an uncle she had never met had died and left his house and all its contents to her. As she came to survey her inheritance, she noticed a barn behind the house filled with what she determined to be rusted, useless junk. The local attorney who was handling the estate suggested that she might have an auction to turn the unwanted pieces into cash. Leslie agreed. On the day of the sale, the contents of the house and barn were assembled together on the lawn and several people gathered to look over the antiques and other relics left from her long lost uncle. As the sale began, bids were placed on different items until the auctioneer came to what appeared to be a old, rusted motorcycle frame. It was small and dirty and only had one wheel. A man from the back of the crowd shouted, "I'll give you $5,000.00 for that it." Quickly, the auctioneer closed the bidding. When asked later why he offered so much for such an apparently worthless piece of junk, the man explained that it was a frame from a rare motorcycle company that had gone out of business many years ago. And while in its current state it was worthless, when it was cleaned up and reassembled it would be priceless. The value of the item is determined by the value of the exchange.

As children of God, we can sometimes feel worthless. Years of living on our own may have left us battered, scarred and rough around the edges. Those around us cannot seem to see the worth that is trapped inside. But God sees something in us that no one else does. He is willing to make an exchange that transforms the thing of no value into something priceless. He will trade something of value for something that others see as worthless. The Bible tells us that He is willing "to bestow on them a crown of beauty instead of ashes, the oil of joy instead of mourning, and a garment of praise instead of a spirit of despair" (Isaiah 61:3) Do you feel like no one sees what you're really worth? Are you willing to make an exchange with God? If we will give God the broken and useless parts of your life, He will clean them up and reassemble them into something that is priceless.

## DAY FIFTY-TWO

## Seeking and Finding

From the time she was a little girl, Ellen had been called "Eagle Eye". It seemed that she could see things that no one else could see. She'd spot her friends in crowd of people. She could find a bird in a tree or spy a squirrel crossing the street on the power lines. She was great at hunting Easter eggs and no one wanted to play hide and seek with her if she were "it". The thing that Ellen was best at finding was money. It seemed that no matter where she went, she would find a dime or a nickel or a quarter on the ground, under a coffee table, or even in the bushes in front of her school. It was if the money were just laying there waiting for her to notice it. Each time she found money, she would put it in a jar in her room and, over the years, she amassed quite a fortune. As she was finishing college, she was on a date with her boyfriend when she spotted a nickel under a car in a store parking lot. Ellen spied it, then got down on her hands and knees and grabbed it from under the car. Amazed, her boyfriend asked her how she was able to see money everywhere she went. With a smile she replied, "I notice it because I'm paying attention. It's not hard to find it if you're looking for it."

While Ellen's ability to find money may have been based less on talent and more on tenacity, her ability does provide a lesson for the Christ-follower. What we look for, what we focus on, will often dictate what we find. The Bible tells us the story of Magi who came from the east to Israel to find the baby Jesus so that they might worship Him. When asked why they thought the "King of the Jews" would be there, the replied, "We saw his star when it rose and have come to worship him." (Matthew 2:2) They saw a star in the sky and determined that God was trying to talk speak to them. Though the star shown over the heads of thousands of other people every night, only the Magi saw it and understood its meaning and its significance. They saw it because they were looking for it. Have you been looking for signs from God? Or are you too busy to notice? We will never know what hidden treasures are right in front of us until we begin to pay attention and look for them. Then we will find what we have been are looking for all along.

## DAY FIFTY-THREE

## The Seasons Of Life

As an old man, Harlan had experienced the changing of the seasons many times. He knew the joy of seeing one season end, and a new one come forth, each bringing blessing and challenges that must be faced. In winter, he loved gathering with friends and family to celebrate Christmas, New Years, and drawing close to the ones he loved at Valentines' Day, but winter's cold often left a dull ache in his bones. Spring brought the hope of newness of life, but also spring rains, allergies and seemingly endless yard work that had to be done. Summer often meant a time of escape for Harlan, a vacation from school when he was younger and from work when he was grown; a chance to enjoy the great outdoors, but the heat of summer often became overwhelming and intrusive. Before he knew it fall entered the picture and his playtime was over. His thoughts returned to the routines of life. Each season brought Harlan joy to be experience and difficulties to be endured. Throughout the year, he endeavored to capitalize on the opportunities each season provided.

Our lives are lived in seasons as well. The Bible tells us that "To everything there is a season, a time for every purpose under heaven." (Ecclesiastes 3:1) Much like the seasons of each year, the seasons of our lives provide both opportunities for joy along with challenges that must be met. It is up to us to wisely choose to enjoy each season as it comes, because before we long, it will come to an end and a new one will arrive, ripe with new joys and new challenges. Are you making the most of the current season of your life? Do you find yourself too often longing for the past or yearning for the future? Learn to take full advantage of all the seasons of life and you will have found a way to live life to the fullest.

## DAY FIFTY-FOUR

**God's Beauty Makeover**

Gina had always wanted to be beautiful. From the time she was a little girl she had lived in the shadow of her older sister who everyone called "the pretty one". Determined to get an advantage, Gina spent seemingly every cent she had, all in the name of looking good. From hair care to makeup and weight loss programs to plastic surgery, Gina had over the years spent time, energy and money in an attempt to make her exterior look as good as it could. While she knew that the Bible did not require the followers of Christ to bypass the makeup counter or the local gym, in a society where appearance is so fundamental to everything that is done, it was difficult for her to know how to balance the desire to put her best foot forward with the need to follow Godly values. She often felt caught up in the struggle between the temporal and the eternal, between inner beauty which comes from a life lived for God, and outer beauty that comes from a store.

The Lord knows our struggles and has given us help in knowing what to do. In His word, God gives us biblical perspective on our beauty regiments. The prophet Isaiah writes, "How beautiful on the mountains are the feet of those who bring good news, who proclaim peace, who bring good tidings, who proclaim salvation." (Isaiah 52:7) God explains to us that in the eyes of the people to whom we bring the Gospel, that even our feet will be beautiful! And while our feet may not be at the top of our beauty regime, they are deemed lovely by those who hear from us the good news of the grace of God. If our feet are beautiful to them, how much more attractive will the rest of us be? Do you need a beauty makeover? Does your interior beauty outshine the exterior? Begin to pass along the "Good News" to those who need to hear it and you may be surprised how attractive you will become from your head all the way down to your toes.

LIFE LESSON IN THE WORD

## DAY FIFTY-FIVE

### Sports Fans In Heaven

Beau loved sports. Though his playing days ended when he finished high school, he never lost his love for competing. His favorite sport to watch was football, especially college football. Every Saturday from Labor Day to Thanksgiving, Beau would be glued to his television watching, cheering, and even yelling at his favorite team. His whole day was planned around what time the game was to start. Though he never missed a game in the last ten years, he had never been to the stadium and watched his favorite team in person. He had always enjoyed the excitement of seeing the game from his favorite chair in the living room of his house. One year for his birthday, his wife surprised him with tickets to watch his team play their arch rival. And if Beau thought watching the game on television was good, as he entered the stadium and found his seat, the whole experience took on an entirely new meaning. He saw cheerleaders and flag-wavers and thousands of fans milling about waiting for kickoff. Then, out of the tunnel from the other end of the stadium came his team and the crowd rose to its feet and cheered with everything they had. Beau was almost overcome with emotion as he joined the massive throng in celebrating their arrival. His team went on to win the game and Beau never looked at college football the same way again.

While we, here on earth, may enjoy gathering together to watch the exploits of athletes as they strive to win the game, there is a similar gathering going on in heaven. The writer of Hebrews tells us that as we go about the process of exercising our faith, we are "surrounded by a great cloud of witnesses",(Hebrews 12:1) an assembled group of fans who have a vested interest in our earthly pursuits. They are gathered in a large crowd in heaven rooting us on, not to catch a pass or hit a home run, but to stay on the path that leads to righteousness. When we come to a crossroads in our walk with God and we decide to follow His principles, there is a cheer that goes up in heaven from the faithful ones who have gone on before. With the same fervor that we cheer when our sports teams cross the goal line, they cheer us on as we strive to follow Godly principles in our everyday lives. Do you feel like you're living your life alone? Are you tired because the game has gotten difficult? Remember there is a group of witnesses in heaven right now rooting for you to succeed. So, give it everything you have and keep striving toward the win.

# LIFE LESSON IN THE WORD

## DAY FIFTY-SIX

### Turning The Car Around

Carl was a young man from a small town who found himself driving in a large metropolitan area. Dazzled by the hustle and bustle of a big city and somewhat inexperienced at driving, he inadvertently drove his car the wrong way down a one-way street. Though he tried to get over to the right side of the road, he could not avoid coming face to face with the approaching traffic. Despite doing his best to dodge the cars that sped his way, he was unaware of the dangerousness of his situation. Just then, a policeman in a patrol car pulled him over and motioned for him to make his way into a parking lot of a local convenience store. The officer explained his error to him, making sure to fully describe the dangers he would have surely encountered if he continued along his current path. Carl was embarrassed and expressed great remorse for his mistake and apologized profusely to the officer. Feeling sorry him, the officer let him go with a warning, asking him never to do such a thing again. Carl agreed and then, to policeman's surprise, pulled his car out of the parking lot and back out onto the street continuing the wrong way on the same one-way street.

While this story may be amusing, too many modern Christians maneuver their lives like Carl driving his car. Though they may have been unaware of their error and inadvertently found themselves in the dangers of sin, they have been apprehended by the truth of the gospel and confronted with the seriousness of their condition. While they may be embarrassed and ashamed at the choices that lead them to such a predicament, and though they may feel great remorse for what they have done, the Bible tells us that they must repent from their sins. The word "repent" means not only to feel sorry for sin, but turn away from them and continue on a different path. Jesus, when he encountered a woman caught in adultery, said to her, "Neither do I condemn you: go, and sin no more." (John 8:11) His words clearly outline the path of true repentance. While on the one hand he forgave her past indiscretions, he cautioned her to take a new path going forward. Have you had your sins forgiven only to continue on the same road? Do you need to truly repent? If we will embrace the concept of repentance, we will not only have our old ways corrected, but will venture out on a new path to bright and glorious future.

LIFE LESSON IN THE WORD

DAY FIFTY –SEVEN

**And Who Are You?**

    Denise had been the personnel manager at an engineering firm for the last 15 years. She had started when the company was very small and had watched it grow into a thriving business. Now with things going so well, she needed help and needed it fast. That's why she had put an ad in the paper of the local college for a summer intern. She was hoping to draw interest from some of the engineering students that could learn the business and, after graduation, come and be a part in taking the company to the next level. So today she was looking forward to interviewing a young man whom the professors at the university had told her had great potential. But about and hour before the scheduled interview, the receptionist came into her office crying. It seems the receptionist's son had been taken to the emergency room and she was concerned about his condition. Undaunted, Denise told her to go and check on her son, she would make sure the front desk was covered. Right on time, the young intern came through the door for his interview. He walked confidently up to Denise whom he assumed was the receptionist. Without greeting her or even looking at her he told her he was here to see the personnel manager. When Denise asked him who he was, he seemed almost offended that a lowly receptionist would question him. He told her, with an air of superiority that it was none of her business. Needless to say, he did not get the job and Denise still smiles when she remembers the look of shock on his face when she revealed that she was not the receptionist, but the person he had come to see.

    As Christ-followers, it is important to learn a lesson from the college student's mistake. We cannot get so caught up in the details of our own life that we look past those around us. We must remember that though we are God's children and He loves us greatly, He loves others just as much. Though we are special to Him, He lavishes his love on all people equally. Paul, in his letter to the church in Rome, cautioned them to "not think of yourself more highly than you ought" (Romans 12:3) While many think of humility as having a low opinion of themselves, it is really more about moving our own wants and desires from the forefront of our thinking and allowing ourselves to regard other people as equals, equally important, equally valuable, and equally deserving of consideration and respect. Do you always think about what you want or need? Are you dealing with a overinflated view of yourself? Ask God to help you see others as He sees them and before long, you will appreciate the value God has placed in all of His children.

## DAY FIFTY-EIGHT

## Forward Or Backward

Brandon borrowed his friend's boat to spend the day fishing. Though he had little experience around boats, he thought he would take an opportunity to try his luck. He stowed his gear aboard the boat and set about casting off from the dock, but he made one fateful error. He untied the vessel from the dock before climbing aboard. As he stepped from the dock to the unfettered boat, it began to drift from the shore leaving Brandon with one foot on the boat and the other on the dock. Realizing that staying where he was could result in increased pain and possible embarrassment, he had to make a choice. He had to decide to whether to go backward to the safety of the dock and risk losing his opportunity for fun and adventure, not to mention the loss of the boat, or take a chance and leap forward in hopes of resuming his plans for the day.

Similarly, the Christian life is not for the faint of heart. It is a life of going all out in pursuit of the truth. The timid of heart, and those who want to play it safe will never experience the true joy and fulfillment of the adventure of serving God. Much of Jesus' ministry was spent challenging people to leave the safety of the dock and make a leap of faith toward him. He encouraged people to step out and follow him when going along with the crowd would have been so much safer. The Apostle Paul echoes this sentiment in his letter to the church in Philippi when he told them to "press toward the goal to win the prize for which God has called me heavenward." (Philippians 3:14) To pursue God means that we must press forward, leaving the past behind. Are you trying to play it safe? Do you find yourself retreating to the security of the dock? God's desire is that we move forward toward Him, pressing past our fears, and He will make our way safe and take us on the adventure of a lifetime.

## DAY FIFTY-NINE

## **Cleanliness Is Next To God**

As she did the laundry, Sara wasn't sure what her husband was doing all day, but she was fairly sure it wasn't good. It seemed that all of his shirts had food stains on the front of them. She wasn't certain how they got there until they went to dinner with another couple later that week. While she enjoyed her dinner and the conversation, she watched as her husband dropped food on his shirt three different times, each one leaving a mark, even after he wiped it away with his napkin. So as she stood over the washing machine with his shirts in hand, she wondered what to do to get rid of the stain. Then she remembered an ad she had seen on television about a new stain remover that claimed it could clean anything. She had even gotten a sample in the mail. She doused the stained garment in the new cleaner and threw it in to wash. As she pulled the shirts out the washer, she noticed that all the stains were gone. It was as if they had never been soiled at all. So, as her husband went about his day, no matter what spill he came home with, Sara knew she had a sure-fire cure for it.

We, as people, live in a stain-filled world. Though none of us goes out looking to pick up the world's dirt, as we go about our day, we sometimes come home with stains on our souls. God reassures his people that he has a sure-fire cure for that. If we accept Jesus' sacrifice on the cross and allow his blood to redeem us, God promises us that though our sins "are like scarlet, they shall be as white as snow; though they are red as crimson, they shall be like wool." (Isaiah 1:18) No matter how dirty our souls get, God can make them clean. If we ask Him, He can make us sparkle like we had never been soiled at all. Have you picked up some unsightly stains? Are you ready to have them gone forever? Allow God to wash your heart and mind and you will come out fresh and clean and ready for a new and brighter day.

## DAY SIXTY

### Finding The Right Partner

Katie wanted more than anything to be a singer. Every day she would practice trying to make her voice sound like the music she heard in her head, but she could never seem to measure up. She had a good voice, but it wasn't strong enough to be great. Undaunted, she tried out for every solo in the church choir, but they always picked someone else. She even entered a local talent show, but didn't make it past the first round. Frustrated, and on the verge of giving up singing all together, she was walking down the hall at church when she heard a guy singing. She was automatically drawn to the sound. She knew the song and without thinking began to sing a harmony part, when all the sudden everything clicked into place. Her voice melded with his in a way that was almost miraculous. Soon they started singing together and doors began to open. Katie found that when she sang with Rick, all her dreams came true. She realized that, sometimes, finding the right partner is the key to success.

As Christ-followers, we read great stories of God's power and what He was able to accomplish in and through seemingly ordinary people. The stories are so attractive and the promises so real that they seem to fly off the page in our direction. We begin to have visions and dreams of all that God can accomplish with us. Our excitement leads us to make plans and begin the task of striving for greatness, only to find that it is not as easy as it seems. No matter how hard we try in our own strength, we can never attain the greatness we desire. We soon fall short. Disappointed, we are eventually tempted to give up. But scripture reminds us that we are not alone in our struggle. The Bible tells us that "it is God who works in you to will and to act according to his good purpose." (Philippians 2:13) If we partner with God, He will not only make it possible for us to achieve the goals He has set before us, but will give us the desire to pursue those goals until we ultimately find success. Are you trying to do great things for God on your own? Have you grown frustrated with seeing your efforts fall short? In the Bible, God inspires His people with stories of extraordinary accomplishment and awesome displays of power.

Before we can achieve our ultimate desire, we must realize that finding the right partner is the key to success.

# LIFE LESSON IN THE WORD

## DAY SIXTY-ONE

## WWJD or WIIFM?

As soon as Tyler entered the military, he began to learn a new language. He had entered the world of acronyms. An acronym is a word formed by using the first letter of a series of other words. For example, the word SCUBA stands for Self-Contained Underwater Breathing Apparatus, and a device that Modulates and Demodulates information between computers was shortened to MODEM. The government is famous for their acronyms. The Strategic Arms Limitation Talks were renamed SALT by the Reagan administration while the North American Free Trade Agreement became NAFTA under Bill Clinton. Many companies use acronyms to shorten their much longer name into something catchy in the hope that this will allow us to remember them. So, International Business Machines became IBM, Kentucky Fried Chicken became KFC and Minnesota Mining and Manufacturing became 3M. Non-profit Organizations do much of the same. The People for the Ethical Treatment of Animals became, the much easier to remember, PETA, the National Aeronautics and Space Administration is better known as NASA and National Association for the Advancement of Colored People is really NAACP. From an IRA to the NFL, acronyms are found in various pastimes and occupations and are useful to break down something complicated into something manageable and memorable.

There are two acronyms that vie for the attention of Christ followers as well. The first is WIIFM. It stands for "What's In It For Me". It is the question we ask ourselves when we are called upon to give more of ourselves than usual or participate in something that stretches our boundaries. While many of us don't like to admit that we use it, it is the attitude of first resort when we are thinking solely about ourselves. The other acronym we commonly come across in Christian circles is WWJD, which many know means "What Would Jesus Do". It is the attitude of selflessness that each of us as followers of Christ should strive for in our everyday lives. At any moment of any given day WIIFM and WWJD battle for preeminence in our minds, our hearts, and our actions. Jesus told his disciples "I have set you an example that you should do as I have done for you".

(John 13:15) Do the acronyms of your life war for your attention? Are you choosing the right one? Decide today to follow the right acronym, and you will begin to break down the complications of this world in to something manageable and make it memorable as well.

# LIFE LESSON IN THE WORD

## DAY SIXTY-TWO

### God's Hand-Crafted Days

Rosemary smiled as she laid the old quilt across the bed. It was a gift from her grandmother who started making it for her the day she was born. Every time she looked at it, she felt special. She had always liked homemade gifts. Whether it was a quilt sewn by her grandmother or an arts and crafts project made by her children, each one was fashioned by someone she loved with her in mind. She knew the time and attention it took to carefully lay out each artistic creation, the hard work and attention to detail. She imagined what the designer was thinking as they put the finishing touches on their creation. How they must have anticipated, with joy, the look on the recipient's face as the gift was delivered. Because of the sentiment behind each of her handmade gifts, whether crudely constructed or assembled with the intricacy of a master craftsman, Rosemary cherished each one. She received them with great appreciation, knowing that a little piece of the creator came along with them as well.

The Bible tells us that "this is the day the Lord has made" (Psalm 118:24). With His own hands, He fashioned it with us in mind. He lovingly formed it for our benefit and painstakingly designed it, knowing that if we receive it with the sentiment intended we would "rejoice and be glad in it." No matter what the events of this day may bring, whether sadness or joy, adversity or prosperity, rough waters or smooth sailing, we can delight that God has handmade it for us. With His love and care, He will make sure that at the end of it, we are one step closer to completing His plan. Are you tempted to take this day for granted? Have you embraced its possibilities or determined to apprehensively face it with dread and drudgery? In each day that the Lord makes, a little piece of the Creator can be found. So, be filled with joy, knowing that the Giver of all good things has presented you with the gift of this day, created specifically with you mind.

## DAY SIXTY-THREE

### Gliders

In the early days of aviation, as Sir George Cayley experimented and studied the flight of birds, he noticed that certain species would float on air, not flapping their wings, but merely gliding on the wind currents. So, before the mechanized airplane was invented, the glider was born. A glider has no propulsion system of its own, but relies on the power of the wind to keep it aloft. Early pilots simply plunged themselves off of high mountains, while today, gliders are towed to the proper altitude by airplanes. Once set free, the glider soars along on wind currents, moving and swaying in the breeze. The glider pilot must have extensive knowledge of wind patterns. Choosing the right one will mean hours in the sky and a soft landing. Choosing an upper air disturbance with wind gusts and turbulence could cause a disastrous tail spin that could end badly in a crash landing, leading to injury or even death. It is important, therefore, for the glider pilot to be cautious in his choice of wind direction in order to fulfill the purpose of his flight and maintain his own well-being.

We as disciples of Jesus are much like a glider. The book of Acts describes the Spirit of God as a rushing wind. With no propulsion of our own, we must rely on the wind provided by the Holy Spirit to propel us on our journey. Likewise, we must choose wisely the wind that carries us along. The Apostle Paul warned the early church not to be "tossed back and forth by the waves, and blown here and there by every wind of teaching and by the cunning and craftiness of people in their deceitful scheming." (Ephesians 4:14) The successful glider pilot must learn to navigate the wind in order to fulfill the purpose of his flight and maintain his own well-being. Are you trying to fly your glider but can't seem to get off the ground? Have you caught the breeze only to crash and burn? Become familiar with wind patterns of God's Spirit and you will soar high over the earth and its problems and gently glide along on His leading.

# DAY SIXTY-FOUR

## Sleepy Communication

Mia woke up in the middle of the night and started to turn over but couldn't. With her mind in a fog, all she knew was that her right arm was numb. It seemed almost dead. As she lay in the darkness gathering her thoughts, she realized that as she slept, her arm had gotten pinned underneath her and now it, too, had fallen asleep. While some believe this phenomenon occurs when pressure is applied to a particular area for an extended time cutting off blood flow to the affected limb, as a nurse, Mia knew that the problem was more accurately attributed to the nerve cells of the body. As we put pressure on a particular area of the body, we inhibit the sending and receiving of messages from the brain. When communication is hindered, the cells of the body become lifeless and useless, like dead weight to be carried around. Thankfully, Mia's condition was not permanent. As she lay there in her bed, the message pathways of her nervous system began to function, and over a short time, her arm was usable again.

Communication is important in the life of the Christ-follower as well. Often times we are tempted to let the pressures of life get to us, making it hard for us to communicate with the Head of our faith, our Lord Jesus. When communication is hindered, we can become lifeless and useless, numb to our circumstances. We become dead weight to be carried around. But like the limb that has fallen asleep, there is hope for our soul. The Bible tells us that we should "pray continually" (1 Thessalonians 5:17). Prayer is simply communication with God, and while we may not be able to speak to God on a continual basis, we can make sure that the lines of communication are always open and the pathways are always clear. Then we will be assured that our spirit will never "fall asleep". Are you feeling sluggish in your life with Christ? Do you feel like dead weight when you want to be alive and useful? Check the communication pathways between you and God and make sure that nothing has impeded them. If you do, you'll always be a useful limb for Him.

## DAY SIXTY-FIVE

## Got You On My Mind

Isaac was a young man in love. Though he had met the girl almost two years ago, and had been friends for some time, they had only been dating for a few months. Isaac found the whole thing very interesting. He had always pictured himself dating and eventually marrying a raven-haired beauty with features that were just as dark as her hair. However, the girl he had fallen head over heals for was fair-skinned beauty with deep blue eyes and flowing red hair. As the relationship grew more serious, the oddest thing began to happen. It seemed that no matter where Isaac went, he saw red-headed people, every one of them reminding him of his beloved. Though red-heads only make up an average of 2% of the population, for Isaac, they seemed to be all over the place. He saw them at the gas station, at the mall, at the movies and even at church. While the population of red-heads did not change, he noticed them more. Isaac experienced a common phenomenon. You see, whatever we are thinking about, whatever we are looking for, we will eventually see. Since Isaac had redheads on his mind, he noticed them more often, where before he would have passed them by.

This phenomenon is common to the people of God as well. If we will focus our attention on God and what He is doing in the world around us, we will see Him in every area of our lives and His handiwork will be ever before us. Though God's involvement in our lives will not have changed, our awareness of His presence will. The Bible tells us that if "you seek the Lord your God, you will find him if you seek him with all your heart and with all your soul." (Deuteronomy 4:29) When we look for God, when we train our mind and our spirit to be alert for Him, we will surely notice Him like we never have before. We will see Him everywhere we go and in every situation we encounter. Are you looking for God? Do you have Him on your mind with the same infatuation as a young man in love? Remember that whatever we are thinking about, whatever we are looking for, we will eventually see. If we want to see God, we must train our eyes to look for Him and before long we will notice Him more often, where before we might have passed Him by.

## DAY SIXTY-SIX

### God and Leftovers

Patricia looked in the refrigerator hoping to find an idea of what to prepare for dinner, but all she could see were leftovers. Leftovers, as everyone knows, are the bits of food left over from a lunch or dinner that are saved to be eaten later. She decided that tonight she would collect the leftovers and make a meal out of the smorgasbord of options. While she was pleased with herself for her economical idea, she was certain her family would be less than excited because, as most everyone will agree, leftovers are often not as good the second time as they were originally. They often lose something in the storage and reheating process that affects the taste and texture of the meal. While leftovers might be acceptable for a family dinner, Patricia would certainly never serve them to guests or other visitors to her home. To do so would be to run the risk of breaking a social boundary and offending her guests. For those who are important to her, she presented her best, most finely prepared dishes to show her guests how special they were to her.

Likewise, God does not want our leftovers. He asks us to give him our best. God gave His people a command to honor Him "with your wealth, with the firstfruits" (Proverbs 3:9) Firstfruits were the choicest and finest portions of the crops and livestock that the people of God could possess. God's desire for us, like the people of Israel, is that we give Him the best of our time, our talent and our treasure. He wants to know how special He is to us. If we are not careful, we will shortchange Him and give Him the leftover fragments of these gifts after we have spent them pursuing our own desires. We will run the risk of offending Him by not giving our best, but saving only the scraps for Him; mere fragments of what we have leftover. Are you giving God your best? When it comes to God, do find that there is nothing left? Make it a point today to show God how special He is to you by reserving the most preeminent portions of yourself and your gifts for Him and you will be amazed how much better your life will be.

## DAY SIXTY-SEVEN

### Listening For God

Jimmy had lived in the same small farming town all his life. Every year he watched as groups of farms hands worked in the barns stacking hay. One day, as they were on their way to lunch, one of the men noticed that he had lost his watch. It was a gift from his father and very precious to him. He and the other farm hands searched the barn but could not find the watch. Discouraged, they left for lunch. Just then, Jimmy happened by and noticed what the men were doing. He went into the barn and in just a few minutes came back out with the man's watch in his hand. As he presented the farm hand with his prize watch, the man asked him how he found it. Jimmy said, "I went into the barn and lay down on the floor and got very quiet. After a while, I was able to hear the ticking of the watch. The sound led me right to it."

Many people ask how to know the will of God in their lives. They earnestly desire to hear His voice. They work hard, stressing and fretting but only hear silence. They walk away discouraged and downhearted. The Bible tells us to hear God's voice we must "be still and know that I am God." (Psalm 46:10) If you will quiet our minds and hearts and focus on Him, God will speak to us and we will be able to find Him, just like Jimmy found the watch. Scripture tells us that God does not speak in a blustering wind or in great fire, or in the fury of the earth. He speaks in a still, small voice. Are you straining to hear from God and getting nowhere? Do you find yourself frustrated and confused? Remember we can only hear God speak when we are still. Then, we will hear His voice; we will find Him and know that He is God.

# LIFE LESSON IN THE WORD

## DAY SIXTY-EIGHT

### Living Your True Identity

As Wesley came back from the store, he stopped by his mailbox to get the mail. With his hands full grocery bags and junk mail, a letter slipped from his grasp and fell to the ground. He didn't notice it and even if he had, he wouldn't have thought much about it. He would have simply picked it up. Soon, that seemingly harmless envelope would change Wesley's life for the next few years. It all started when he got his credit card statement later that month. He noticed charges on his account that he had not made. Soon after, he began to get calls from debt collection agencies regarding unpaid balances on accounts he had never opened. When he checked his credit information, there were loans and credit cards and debts that he knew nothing about. That missing letter was an offer to open up a new charge account and someone had taken full advantage of the opportunity it provided. To his great pain and embarrassment, Wesley realized that someone had stolen his identity.

In Bible times, especially in the Old Testament, people were identified by the meaning of the name their parents gave them. Because of this, Jabez was a "pain" and Jacob was a "deceiver", while Noah was a "comfort" and David was "beloved". Oftentimes, people lived up to the name with which they were identified. Moses really did "deliver" his people and Solomon was "peaceful". In modern times, identity takes on a whole new meaning. People can have their original identity stolen to be replaced by one that is tied to what they've done. The one who started out as a nice young girl can soon be identified as loose. The guy who doesn't fit in is labeled a thug and the kid in school who has trouble reading is called slow or dumb. In ancient times, if some significant event took place in a person's life, they got a new name, a new identity. They were not then known by what went before, but could forge a new life. Likewise, we do not have to be identified by what we have done, but by who we can be. We can start over and live life anew. The Bible tells us that "in Christ Jesus you are all children of God through faith." (Galatians 3:26) As we follow Jesus, we take on the identity of children of God and discard the labels given to us by others. Has someone stolen your real identity? Have you been labeled because of what you have done? The events of our past need not define us. As children of God, we can throw off our old life and reclaim our identity in Hm.

LIFE LESSON IN THE WORD

## DAY SIXTY-NINE

## Conventional Wisdom VS God's Wisdom

While Brooke had heard of what is known as "conventional wisdom", she was not always convinced. She understood that it is the process used to determine what people or things will do well in a given arena based on what has taken place in the past. She was also aware that while past success can be a wonderful indicator of future success, there are times when conventional wisdom can be terribly wrong. It was conventional wisdom that cut Michael Jordan from the high school basketball team and Elvis Presley from the choir because they weren't good enough. It was conventional wisdom that told Bill Gates that his little idea of the personal computer would never work, that television, the satellite, and the internet were all fads that would soon die out. Since human wisdom is based upon the natural world, it can be an accurate indicator of the way things are right now, but often fails to correctly gauge the way things can be. Because of this, Brooke began to search for wisdom that was more supernatural.

While we as people strive to make sense of the world around us using our God-given intellect, we must understand that our wisdom is limited. We must realize that God's wisdom is unlimited, unfathomable, and often times, very unconventional. In the business world, they call it "thinking outside the box". In the Christian world, we call it "thinking like God". 1 Corinthians tells us that God "will destroy the wisdom of the wise". It says that that He has chosen "the foolish things of the world to confound wise" and "the weak things of the world to confound the strong". (1 Corinthians 1:27) The pages of the Bible are full of stories of how God raised people up from out of nowhere to become the prominent leaders of their day. He has a way of making champions out of underdogs and over-comers out of the ones nobody ever believed would amount to anything. Has conventional wisdom told you that your dream is impossible? Do you feel like you will never make it? Hold onto what God says about you. With Him, you can rise from the bottom to the top and come out victoriously no matter the odds.

## DAY SEVENTY

### **Drifting**

Gary had always loved the water. It seemed like every weekend he could be found down at the ocean swimming, boating or fishing. That's why no one had trouble believing the story about the time that he rowed his boat out into a large lake near the ocean in order to do some fishing. The sun was warm and the wind off of the water was so comforting that after some time in the boat, Gary fell asleep. While he slept, the tide went out and his boat drifted very far from shore. When he awoke, he found himself adrift, and the shore that had been very close, was now a small speck in the distance. He rubbed his eyes and asked "Who moved the earth?" The reality, of course, was that the earth hadn't moved at all, but unbeknownst to Gary, he had drifted away from shore.

There are times that we go through seasons where we sense God's power very strongly in our lives. We feel like He is as close as our next breath. Still there are other times, when through stress, or distraction, or our own loss of focus, we can drift away and God's presence which was once so close now seems a million miles away. If God seems far away from you today, keep in mind that He didn't move. Thankfully, the solution to our dilemma is simple. The Bible promises the believer that if you will "come near to God and He will come near to you." (James 4:8) We need to aim our boat at the shore and go back to safe waters. He will be with us if we will just row our boat toward Him and anchor our lives near Him. Are you feeling lost or alone? Does God seem far away now? Just call out His name and begin to paddle toward the shore. He is waiting on the dock to greet you.

LIFE LESSON IN THE WORD

DAY SEVENTY-ONE

## Insecure Security

The minute Corey walked into his house, he knew something was wrong. The door he was sure he had locked was ajar and as he made his way into the living room, he immediately noticed several things were missing. His television and laptop were both gone. As he checked the rest of the house, his wife's jewelry had been taken along with the envelope of cash that he kept in his sock drawer. Along with the feeling of being violated, Corey quickly realized how insecure the world we live in can be. To combat his growing anxiety, he bought locks to protect his property, insurance to protect his finances, and alarm systems to protect his life and the lives of his family. Despite his best efforts, he still lived in anticipation of what might happen. Though he barricaded himself behind security doors and access codes, Corey came to realize that though the precautions he took made him safer, they were no guarantee of safety. He could hunker down in hopes of insulating himself from the insecurity of the world, but no amount of hardware could ever really make him feel secure again.

As believers in Jesus, we are not immune to the pressure of insecurity. We may feel the same stress and experience the same tension as those around us. But we have one thing the world does not have. We have hope. Jesus told his followers to "store up treasure in heaven, where moth and rust do not destroy, and where thieves do not break in and steal." (Matthew 6:20) He said there is a place where we could invest our time, talent and treasure where it will remain safe despite what politicians, the economic indicators or the crime statistics tell us. Are you perplexed as to how to protect yourself from harm? Do the current instabilities in our world have you stressed? Be sure to invest in a secure place that is safe from this world and its troubles. Remember "where your treasure is, there your heart will be also." (Matthew 6:21)

## DAY SEVENTY-TWO

### Being God's Hands

As a medic in the army and after becoming a surgeon back home, Tony's hands had saved lives. He knew they were one of the most useful parts of the human body. With the exception of the organs that keep us alive, our hands are the most important parts we have. They seem to factor into every area of life, from making a living, to cooking and eating, to pursuing our hobbies and pastimes. Our hands do it all. Not only are our hands useful in every area of our lives, they tell the story of our activities. From the mechanic with stubborn grease wedged in the creases of his fingers, to the fisherman whose hands still smell of the catch, to the farmer and the construction worker with hardened calluses to prove their day's hard work, our hands contain the residue of the places we've been and things we've done.

Hands are important to God as well. With them we can provide comfort to a friend, cup the face of a child or reach out those in need. Solomon wrote "Whatever your hand finds to do, do it with all your might. (Ecclesiastes 9:10) The most important thing we can do with our hands is give honor and praise to God. The Apostle Paul gave Timothy the command to "lift up holy hands in prayer." (1 Timothy 2:8) As we worship our Heavenly Father, our hands take on the residue of His presence so that they can be an extension of His hands and be a blessing to all those around us. What have you been doing with your hands? Are they exalting God? Remember, you can tell much about a person by what they do with their hands. God wants us to use ours to bring glory and honor to His name.

# LIFE LESSON IN THE WORD

## DAY SEVENTY-THREE

### Summertime Rain Showers

As Luke stood on the deck behind his house and looked up in to the sky, he could tell that a thunderstorm was coming. It had been a particularly warm summer day, and as the temperature outside had risen, so had the humidity level. By mid afternoon, the warm air was so thick with humidity that it enveloped everyone like a blanket, making even the slightest movement miserable. Now it was late in the afternoon and the temperature had dropped slightly as a cool breeze began to blow. The hot stagnant air that was pregnant with moisture was about to give birth to rain. As the rain began to fall, it gave rise to a thundershower. The clouds almost seemed in a hurry to empty themselves of the water that they held onto for so long. The most amazing part for Luke was that after the rain, when everything had settled back down, the heavy stagnant air was replaced by a light freshness, as the earth seemed breathe a sigh of relief from the oppressive heat and humidity that had held it trapped.

From time to time, we as people function the same as the earth on a hot, humid day. As the temperature of our lives goes up, we cling to what we believe are the life-sustaining essentials, only to find that, instead of helping us, they only serve to make us more uncomfortable. With everything around us feeling sticky and unpleasant, we need the cool breeze of God in our lives that allows us to let go of the things that are making us miserable. The Bible tells us to "cast all your anxieties on him because he cares for you." (1 Peter 5:7) If we let him, God will be the gentle wind on a steamy day that allows us to breathe a sigh of relief as we unload the burden that we have been carrying and experience life afresh and anew. Are you all hot and bothered? Do you long for refreshment from the oppressive heat of your life? Seek God today and His soothing breeze will blow your way, bringing with it relief from the summertime blues.

## DAY SEVENTY-FOUR

## Finding The Escape Hatch

It seemed to his parents that Brad had been born to be a pilot. He was fascinated by anything that flew. As a young boy he built model airplanes, and when he got his first radio-controlled airplane, he was hooked. He studied endlessly and seemed to know everything there was to know about airplanes. So no one was surprised when he joined the Air Force and went to flight school. While there, he learned about advanced aerodynamics, and how to fly a jet. Everything was fine until it came to bail-out training. Sitting in a simulated cockpit chair, Brad was shown how to locate and deploy the ejection seat. "Why do we need this?" he asked. His instructor explained. "If there is a problem with the airplane that you cannot correct, if you find yourself in a situation that is too difficult for you to manage, this device will get you out of the plane and save your life."

While many Christ-followers will never deal with the difficulties and dangers of a fighter pilot, we are faced with trials and temptations that have the potential to cause us great harm. Our Heavenly Father knows this and has set up a system that will allow us to "eject" when we find ourselves in a temptation that looks to defeat us. The Bible tells us that, "God is faithful; he will not let you be tempted beyond what you can bear. But when you are tempted, he will also provide a way out." (1 Corinthians 10:13) As we make our way through life and temptation comes looking for us, we will quickly find ourselves in a battle. Though the raging of the struggle can become intense, we know that, even as the enemy looks to destroy us, if we look to Him, God will make a way for us to escape. Are you battling with a temptation that looks too overwhelming? Do you feel like there is no way out? God has an escape hatch in every temptation so that if there is a problem that you cannot correct, if you find yourself in a situation that is too difficult for you to manage, He will get you out of it and save your life.

LIFE LESSON IN THE WORD

## DAY SEVENTY-FIVE

### Role The Credits

Glen had always had always loved movies. He was fascinated by the opportunity to travel to far off lands or experience life in a different time period through the flickering images on the screen. Though deep down, he knew he would never be a part of Hollywood, he was enthralled with everything about the movies, from the actors and directors to the supporting cast and crew that made the film possible. While most people never read the credits at the end of a movie, choosing to use that time to exit the theater instead, Glen loved to know everything he could about the inner workings of the job of making movies. After only a little while, it was clear to him that the movie-making process is a team effort. Even though most of the recognition for a film's success often goes to the main actors or even the director, shooting a movie is the culmination of hard work from the supporting cast. From those who run the cameras, lights and sound to those who make costumes and sets, everyone's job is a vital and necessary. Without the contribution of technicians, craftsmen, and support staff, the process would grind to a halt and failure would be inevitable.

The same can be said for the vision God has for our lives. Living out our faith, if done correctly is a team sport. Without the efforts of fellow believers in our lives, we are often doomed to failure. God said of Adam, "It is not good for man to be alone." (Genesis 2:18) Solomon echoed this sentiment when he said "Two are better than one, because they have a good return for their work. If one falls down, his friend can help him up. But pity the man who falls and has no one to help him up!" (Ecclesiastes 4:9-10) God set up this world so that we would need each other. We as people cannot even reproduce a single human life without the contribution of another person. If God made it so that we could not bring about something as basic as that by ourselves, how do we hope to accomplish the glorious vision and plan that He has for us without the involvement of others? Are you a loner? Do you find yourself trying to do everything on your own? We must realize that we were not meant to tackle life's challenges alone. As we involve others in our walk with God by asking them for the help and support we desperately need, our life will turn out to be a runaway success.

LIFE LESSON IN THE WORD

## DAY SEVENTY-SIX

## God & The Game Show

Miguel knew that reality television, as it is called, was extremely popular with viewers from all over the world. He knew that people tune in each week to watch ordinary people go through extraordinary circumstances for the promise of cash, prizes and a modicum of notoriety. He knew his best opportunity to be one of those people was to appear on a game show. There he could dazzle viewers with his vast knowledge on a variety of topics leaving some to wonder how anyone could know so much. He hoped to come back day after day, week after week to defend his title showing a depth and breadth of knowledge that would leave others astounded, defeating his opponents and retaining his place as a champion. People would marvel at his vast intellect as they realized that not everyone has the ability to remember the answers and recite them with that same speed and expertise. The audience would celebrate his game show success as a testimony to their appreciation for information and knowledge. Just then, he woke up in his favorite chair and realized he had fallen asleep again while watching Jeopardy.

We, as disciples of Jesus, have a similar appreciation for knowledge. As we make our way through this life, we travel dimly lit paths with blind curves and faded horizons. The Apostle Paul referred to looking at a "poor reflection as in a mirror." (1 Corinthians 13:12) We never seem to know what each day will bring. We strive to make sense of life's questions and look for answers that never seem to come. But in scripture, Jesus tells his disciples that the Holy Spirit will "guide you into all truth." (John 16:13) As you and I follow the leading of the Holy Spirit, He will feed us the answers to the deep questions of life and allow us to come out in the winner's circle. He will cause the profound truths of life to come into full view. Do you ever feel like life is a puzzle with no clear solution? Are you facing questions that are just too hard for you to answer? Call out to the God who holds the reservoir of all truth in the palm of His hand and He will get you past the competition and into life's great bonus round.

## DAY SEVENTY-SEVEN

### Turning Sorrow Into Joy

In her 9th month of her first pregnancy, Ashley felt like an over-inflated beach ball. She was uncomfortable no matter what she did. When she stood, her back began to hurt and her feet would swell. When she sat down, her girth made breathing difficult and movement impossible. As the delivery date drew close, she marked off the days on the calendar, not only for the anticipation of the baby that would be born but also the loss of the load she was carrying. She felt trapped in her own body and soon the joy of bringing a new life into the world was replaced by sorrow for her situation. All that changed at two o'clock in the morning just one day prior to her due date. She felt a pain like she had never felt before. It seemed to radiate from her knees all the way up to her chin. And just when she thought it would never stop, it actually did. It went away for ten minutes, but then it started all over again. Knowing this was the sign that the baby was on its way, Ashley woke her husband and they headed to the hospital. Over the next fifteen hours, Ashley experienced more pain than she had endured in all her life combined. Exhausted and sweaty, the doctor told her one last push would do it. Summoning all her strength, she was so relieved when she heard her newborn son cry for the first time. As she held him and looked into his little face, all the pain and discomfort was washed away from her mind and she basked in the joy of her husband and baby and the life they would have together.

The exchange of joy for pain is a common theme in the life of the Christ-follower. God has the same ability to turn tragedy into triumph. Scripture tells us that "all things work together for good to those who love God and are called according to His purpose." (Romans 8:28) This means that no matter how bad a situation appears on the outside, God has the ability to bring good from it. He can take the most difficult of circumstances and reshape for our benefit. While we may be hard-pressed to see any good in the difficulties we face, in His timing, God has the capacity to extract something miraculous from what we might think of as misfortune. Over time, what was originally thought of as a bother can be refashioned into a blessing. Are you facing hard times? Do you think that nothing good could ever come of your struggle? Allow God to work in your life and He will turn your sorrow into joy, and you, and those who know you, will be better for it.

## DAY SEVENTY-EIGHT

### Following The Program

From the first time that he touched one, Paul was convinced that personal computers were one of the greatest inventions mankind had ever conceived. With them, he was able to conduct business, reach out to friends, write stories, make movies and even play games. While computers can be a wonderful tool for so many things, they don't run on their own agenda. They run on a program, a prefabricated set of commands that their creator fashioned, which provides detailed instructions as to how to operate in any given set of circumstances. If the computer follows these instructions, then great things are possible. If the computer fails to follow the program, productivity plummets, and the dreams and desires of the user are hampered or even stopped. If the computer's inability to follow its prescribed directives persists, it falls into disrepair and must be reprogrammed or even discarded. Only computers that follow their programming are useful.

The Bible is God's program. In it, He lays out principles that serve as a set of instructions, giving direction to the user on how to operate through life. He provides us with directives as to what to do, what not to do and even tips on what to do if something goes wrong. His desire is that "you remain in me and my words remain in you" (John 15:7) If we follow His program, we will be able to do great things. Our lives will become a framework for endless possibilities where anything is achievable. But if we fail to follow the Designer's program, we will fall into dysfunction and eventual disorder that will lead to ultimate destruction. We make the choice. Do you feel like your life is like a hard drive running with no output? Did you write your own program only to find that it was corrupt? Start today to reprogram your life according to God's word and you'll soon find your system will begin working at maximum efficiency.

LIFE LESSON IN THE WORD

## DAY SEVENY-NINE

## Keeping A Positive Outlook

As a part of his education, Randy was asked to volunteer at a retirement home. Hesitantly he agreed, but only to fill his requirements. When he arrived at the home, he saw elderly men and women in varying degrees of activity. He was particularly drawn to Amos, an older gentleman whose face radiated with a broad smile. As Randy approached him, Amos looked up with a grin and engaged him in conversation. Over the weeks that followed, as Randy visited his older friend, he noticed that despite physical and financial struggles, Amos endured his fate with a positive outlook. After a while, curiosity overcame him and Randy asked the older gentleman about his amazing ability to stay positive in the midst of overwhelming difficulties. Amos explained that as a younger man he had served in the army and was sent into combat. "Every day", he said, "I woke up realizing that someone I didn't know was trying to kill me. Since I survived that ordeal, I determined that any day I wake up and no one is trying to kill me, is going to be a good day."

We, as people, face challenges every day. We encounter obstacles both big and small. In the midst of our day-to-day struggles, we may be tempted to lose perspective on the bigger picture, the eternal perspective. We must realize that the outlook from which we view our current condition will many times determine its final outcome. The Apostle Paul reiterated this point when he told the church in Rome that "our present sufferings are not worth comparing to the glory that will be revealed in us."(Romans 8:18) God's plan for us is much bigger than the life we lead today. As we make our way along the path, we will encounter some difficulties, but if we maintain a positive outlook, we will not only carry through them but triumph over them and emerge on the other side stronger and better. Are you tempted to get lost in the issues you face today? Has difficulty turned your faith into doubt? Remember that God has a plan for each of us and that even though this day may have its share of trouble, we can look at our struggles with positive outlook knowing that, despite the problems, today can be a good day.

## DAY EIGHTY

## **The Winter Of Our Discontent**

As she plopped herself down on the couch, Phoebe was bored and frustrated. With nothing on television and not much to do, she started watching an infomercial about the latest revolutionary product. The more she watched, the more she determined that she had to have what they were selling. Soon she found herself dialing the phone with her credit card in hand. It wasn't that she needed it, but Phoebe, like many in our current culture, was looking to overcome a mind-set of discontentment. Some seem to always be in a never-ending search for happiness and fulfillment, a trouble-free place where all the areas of life are just to our liking and everything is good. Believing the advertisers' promise, we search for contentment in the latest things, the newest toy, the most popular destinations that will "change our lives". Yet, no matter how hard many of us seek, we cannot seem to find it. While one part of our lives may be going well, we find another part that is lagging behind. We then quickly shift our focus and attention on the things that aren't working properly in hopes of making them right, only to find we have neglected still another area whose deficits now clamor for our attention. Like a leaf caught in a tornado, we are blown from one thing to another in the belief that someday we will fix all the problems and live in a world of contentment, not realizing that, if we trust in our own power to create satisfaction, that day will never come.

For the Christ-follower, contentedness is achieved not because the circumstances of their lives have dictated it, but because of closeness of their relationship with God. The Apostle Paul writing to the church in Philippi states it clearly. "I have learned the secret of being content in any and every situation, whether well fed or hungry, whether living in plenty or in want." (Philippians 4:12) God promises us a life that is filled with peace in the midst of our current chaos, not because all things are under control but in spite of it. This peace, however, does not come to us naturally. Paul reminds us that he has "learned to secret of being content." We must allow the Spirit of God to teach us His ways so that we begin to experience His fulfillment. Only then, will we ever know true satisfaction and joy and live in state of contentment. Are you trying to manufacture satisfaction on your own? Are you chasing a dream of inner peace only to find you're living in a whirlwind of unmet expectations? Start today to apply God's principles for contented living and soon you will breathe easier, live freer and love fuller in the life He has given.

## DAY EIGHTY-ONE

## Success Is No Accident

With his golf ball laying in the middle of the sand trap, Riley was less than happy. As he trudged in the bunker, he hoped he could just get the ball out of the sand and onto some grass. That is why no one was more surprised than he was when as the ball left his club head, popped up in the air, landed on the green and rolled in to the hole. While he was overjoyed at his accomplishment, he knew that it had more to do with luck than skill. And though his shot was exciting, he understood that only with practice would it be something he could do on a regular basis. Riley understood that true success is the long-term result of small, deliberate, and persistent decisions made on a daily basis. It is not an overnight sensation, but the product of hard work and right decisions made over the course of time. While some believe that success is reserved for the lucky or great talented, or meant only for a select few, true success is not accidental. It is the junction where desire meets determination. It is the process of growing, striving and maturing that leads to the achievement of ultimate success. While we may unintentionally find some measure of accomplishment, we will only find true success after we try and fail and try yet again.

Success in the Christian walk is no different. It is less a matter of luck and opportunity and more about determination and diligence. If we are going to be all that God intends us to be, we must be ready to do the work. Persistence and tenacity are key elements in any successful endeavor. In his letter to the church at Philippi, the Apostle Paul instructs them to "continue to work out your salvation with fear and trembling". (Philippians 2:12) Sanctification is the process of becoming like Jesus. While it is necessary to the success of every Christ-follower, it not something that can be accomplished overnight, nor can it be achieved by accident. It is only possible if we commit ourselves to deliberately and persistently making Godly decisions a daily basis. God's desire is that we roll up our sleeves and do what must be done, not for just a moment, but continuously. While it is encouraging to see progress, we cannot rest on our laurels and think that we have arrived. Only when we commit ourselves and all that we have will we see the Kingdom of God advanced. Do you find yourself gaining ground, only to lose it again? Do you take two steps forward and one step back? Keep working toward your goal. Remember we should not become "weary in doing good, for at the proper time we <u>will</u> reap a harvest if we do not give up." (Galatians 6:9)

## DAY EIGHTY-TWO

## Moving The Immovable

As Tracy left the orthodontists office, she ran her tongue along her new braces. She knew that for the next few months, her braces would have a tough job as they tried to rearrange her teeth, which she realized are some of the most solid parts of her body. From biting into fruit to tearing meat, her teeth were strong and solid, yet the orthodontist told her that even as solid as her teeth were, they could be moved. He applied braces to each tooth to straighten the crooked areas of her smile. With small but constant pressure over time, the teeth that seemed entrenched in her gums, would be easily repositioned into perfect alignment. Though the progress would be almost imperceptible to the eye, over time, persistence would pay off and eventually the difference would be evident. The doctor assured her she would be amazed at the change that had taken place.

Often in our lives we face difficulties and struggles that seem overwhelming. We deal with obstacles that loom large before us and may appear to us as immoveable. When we encounter these deep-rooted issues, we may be compelled to believe that the situation is hopeless. We may even feel like giving up. But like the doctor who moves our crooked teeth, God has a plan for fixing what has gone wrong. He tells us to "continue in what you have learned and have become convinced of". (2 Timothy 3:14) Only by adhering to God's word and remaining in God's plan will we see the immovable moved. With small but constant pressure over time, the crooked can be made straight. Though our progress at times may seem insignificant, if we remain in Him, we will be amazed at the change that has taken place. Are you facing a stubborn roadblock? Do you feel like you are caught between a rock and hard place? Continue to follow God's leading and in time you will see all things brought into alignment.

LIFE LESSON IN THE WORD

## DAY EIGHTY-THREE

## My Heavenly Back-Up

Valarie was one smart woman. While working as a paralegal at a law firm, she was also trying to finish her MBA. That made what happened all the more strange. She was writing a paper on her laptop while sitting in the college library. Just as she went to save her work, her computer malfunctioned. In an instant, she not only lost all the data from the paper she was writing, as well as the research materials she had stored to write her big thesis. She also lost her pictures, her music, and her financial records. All of them were gone. Frantically, she took her laptop to her friend who ran a computer repair shop. After looking over the machine, he gave her the bad news. The hard drive was damaged beyond repair. "I hope you backed up all your files.", he said with a smirk, but she hadn't. What she failed to realize is that even the best that man has to offer will eventually fail. That is why we need a safe place to secure the things that are most important to us.

Many of us have experienced Valarie's plight. We have trusted in our own abilities only to find that what we thought was secure, proved later to be unreliable; what we thought would never fail us turned out to be fallible. The Bible gives an answer that will bring us hope. "Trust in the LORD with all your heart and lean not on your own understanding; in all your ways submit to him, and he will make your paths straight." (Proverbs 3:5-6) The promise is that though our best efforts may fall short, God's ways are foolproof. Though our tactics may fail, God's power is perfect. If we trust in Him, He will never fail us. Are you putting your faith in man-made structures? Have you trusted in things that only let you down? Allow God to be your back up and the things that are most important to you will always remain secure.

# DAY EIGHTY-FOUR

## Our Christian Mascot

Jordan was the mascot of his high school football team. Every game, he climbed into his foam costume and excited the crowd, while trying to spur his team onto victory. He knew that the mascot serves as the center point of the team's identity, while giving the fans an icon to rally around. When choosing a mascot, it is common to choose one that not only reflects the values of the team and their potential to win the game, but one that will strike fear in the hearts of your opponents. Some teams choose animals that are fierce like lions, tigers or bears. Others choose birds that can swoop down and cause havoc like eagles, falcons, or hawks. While some choose groups known for their toughness like Vikings, Indians, or Pirates. Still other teams choose their mascot based upon what they find in their surroundings like terrapins, ducks, or buckeyes. The most confusing mascots are the ones that don't seem to fit into any category such as supersonics, chargers, and even the tide. While mascots are a fun part of most any sport, they are an important reminder of who the team is and all they stand for.

As Christ-followers, we are given a mascot to represent who we are in Jesus. We are called God's sheep. The sheep serves as a good representation of what God's desire is for us. Sheep are not fierce or dangerous. They are neither fast nor crafty. Sheep only have two characteristics that allow them to survive. First, sheep are really good at following. Cattle are driven from behind. Sheep are lead from the front. They will line up behind their leader and follow him wherever he goes, never questioning or quarrelling, just following. Secondly, sheep know the voice of their shepherd. Jesus said, "My sheep listen to my voice; I know them, and they follow me." (John 10:27) Though they will scatter if someone else tries to call them, sheep will follow the voice of their shepherd. Are you cheering the wrong mascot? Have you embraced your inner sheep? Remember God's desire is that we learn to hear His voice and follow Him along life's path. If we do, we will represent him and ourselves very well.

LIFE LESSON IN THE WORD

## DAY EIGHTY-FIVE

## These Are The Good Old Days

Courtney never seemed happy about anything. Despite countless blessings, she never seemed content with the way things were. She had a nice house and a good job. She had a husband who loved her and kids who adored her. She was respected at church and even helped in the nursery, but it never seemed to matter. Her constant misery concerning her current life often drove her to remember fondly the events of her past. She could regularly be found looking through old photo albums and yearbooks, reliving the glory days of her past and trying to figure out how such a bright future had gone so wrong. One day, as she was visiting with her mother, she began to tell of how hard her life was and how she wished she could go back to the past. Her mother looked at her with astonishment and asked, "Why?" Courtney told her mother that she thought often about the past and how much fun she had back then. She remembered a time when the family had gone on a camping trip to the Ozarks. They had had a great time fishing, hiking and swimming. Courtney's mother was taken aback. She informed her daughter that her memory may be bit off. Her mother did remember that trip. Courtney had spent the whole time complaining about the bugs by the campfire, the blisters on her feet from the hike and the algae growing on top of the water in the pond. It had not been a great time but more of a disaster.

As we look to the past, our memories often remove the difficult and painful passages, leaving only the good parts. As we deal with difficulties in the present, we may be fooled into believing that the "good old days" were better than they actually were. Worse yet, time spent reliving the past may cause us to miss the good days that are happening right in front of us. Jesus warned us that anyone who "puts a hand to the plow and looks back is fit for service in the kingdom of God." (Luke 9:62) While we can enjoy occasionally reminiscing, we must remember that the events of our past are still in the past, never to be resurrected again. We cannot allow ourselves to miss out on the wonderful things that are going on today by living in yesterday. We must embrace the good that God has prepared for us in each day. Are you stuck in the past? Has your memory of the good old days clouded your judgment of the here and now? We must take time to count our blessings and enjoy the wonder that God has laid before us, so that sometime in the future we can look back on toady and smile.

# LIFE LESSON IN THE WORD

## DAY EIGHTY-SIX

### I've Got A Bad Feeling

Meagan was somewhat nervous as she parked her car and walked into the church. She had not darkened the door of a church in several years, but recent events in her life compelled her to reach out to God once again. She had grown up in church, but in her teens she began to drift from her faith. After high school, she had begun to hang out with a rough crowd and before she knew it, she was doing things that years earlier she would have never believed she would do. She knew what she was doing was wrong but she felt like God would never want her now that she had spent so much time away. She felt guilty about how she was living, but entered the church and found a seat and listened intently to the pastor's message. When he asked for people to come forward, she ran to the front to accept God's offer of forgiveness. In a moment, the weight of her guilt was lifted and she felt brand new. Over the next few months, she turned her life around, reading the Bible, praying and attending church, but occasionally though she had left her old life behind, a feeling of guilt about her past would overcome her and she wondered if anything had really changed at all.

Conviction is the uncomfortable feeling we get when we know we've done something wrong. It is a mechanism that the Holy Spirit uses to urge us to return to God and make things right. It is difficult and unrelenting, but effective if we heed its message. Once we return to God and repent of our sins, God says that He forgives and cleanses us from all unrighteousness. However, the enemy of our souls is not so forgiving. His desire is to make us sweat a little more over our misdeeds. That feeling is called condemnation. While to us it may feel very similar to conviction, it is feeling bad about sins of the past that God has forgiven and forgotten. The Bible tells us that "there is now no condemnation for those who are in Christ Jesus". (Romans 8:1) God is not in the business of bringing up old transgressions, but is interested in a healthy relationship with us. Are you haunted by the sins of the past? Are you burdened even though God has set you free? Remember that condemnation does not come from God. It is a trick of the enemy to discourage us and make us feel guilty about the unhealthy and unholy decisions of our past.

Decide today to reject condemnation and live the life of freedom that God has designed for you.

## DAY EIGHTY-SEVEN

## Studying To Pass The Test

Peggy had always had a fear of taking tests. She would get stressed about what she would be asked and wonder if she would know the answers to the questions. She often would ask her youth pastor to pray that she would do well on the test. But what she didn't understand was, like a sponge, the human mind will only give out what is in it. While God may help us remember what we have studied and retrieve it efficiently, He will not circumvent the study process to get out of us what is not already in us. It is the job of the student to study the material carefully and thoroughly to implant the knowledge into the brain until it becomes a very part of who they are. Then, in the time of testing, the knowledge will flow out of them easily and they will experience success.

Like the student, Christ-followers face stress. We encounter times of periodic testing that can be unnerving. We wonder if we will be successful in our endeavor to follow God and His plan for us. Like the student, we must realize that the only thing that will come out of us is what is already in us. We will only be successful if we have taken the time and energy to study the materials in preparation for the test. King David explained it this way. "I have hidden your word in my heart that I might not sin against you." (Psalm 119:11) Are you asking God to give you knowledge for which you have not studied? Have you taken time to read the Book so that you can pass the test? God's goal for us is to live out our Christian lives successfully. But we will never achieve God's best until we first learn His word and make it a very part of who we are, so that in a time of testing, we will be all that He has meant for us to be.

# DAY EIGHTY-EIGHT

## Counting The Cost

In the early to mid 1800's, Martin was an apprentice at the local blacksmith outside of Boston. Though he didn't mind working in the blacksmith shop he dreamed of venturing westward in search of a better life. One day, he decided to leave the relative safety of the city and journey to the Midwest following a promise of free land. Though some made their way to the west coast in search of fortune in the gold mines and boom towns of the pacific coast, Martin settled in farm country just east of St Louis. Martin, like most of these adventurers that moved west found that the task they had undertaken was far less glamorous or exciting than they expected and the struggles associated with their relocation and settlement were much more than they bargained for. Like many people who take on a new challenge, Martin had overestimated the benefits and underestimated the difficulty. Some might say that had he accurately calculated both the rewards and the hazards, he probably wouldn't have ventured out. It is no less important to realize that when the realities of any new adventure set in, we must make a decision to either press on in our efforts or cut our losses and head back to where we began.

Beginning a relationship with God often resembles the trek of our pioneering ancestors. We choose to leave familiar territory to venture out into something unfamiliar in the hope of a better life. And like our pioneering forefathers, many new believers find that they have underestimated the difficulty of living a Godly life in an ungodly world. It is at that moment of realization that we must understand that for every endeavor there are costs that must be paid. Jesus, in addressing his disciples put it this way, "Suppose one of you wants to build a tower. Will he not first sit down and estimate the cost to see if he has enough money to complete it?" (Luke 14:28) Whether building a tower or a new life with God, when the going gets rough, we must take stock of ourselves and determine if we have what it takes to move forward or head back the way we came. Have you begun a life with God only to find that it is not as easy as you imagined? Are you contemplating giving up? Keep in mind that unlike the pioneers who sought a new life in this world with no guarantee of success, Jesus promises that if we count the cost and continue in him, our efforts will be rewarded beyond our wildest dreams not only now, but for all eternity.

## DAY EIGHTY-NINE

## Elements Of True Worship

In her high school chemistry class, Michele learned that Sodium Chloride, or ordinary table salt as it is better known, is made up of two common and somewhat abstract elements. Sodium in its natural form is a yellow powdery substance that reacts violently when mixed with water, while chlorine is an inert gas that is toxic to humans in even small concentrations. Separately they have limited uses and applications. Together they form one of the common building blocks of life. Our bodies crave salt and it is found in all of the many liquids that make up the human form. Salt is an essential part of daily life and was used by ancient peoples to preserve food. Today we use it to bring flavor to much of the things we eat. Without salt, life as we know it would not be possible.

Worship is an essential part of the life of any follower of Jesus. Our spirits crave it. It is fundamental in preserving the health of our spiritual walk and it brings flavor to our daily lives. The Bible tells us that to truly be effective we must "worship in spirit and in truth." (John 4:24) Our worship must contain these two common elements to be powerful and life-giving. Worship that is biblical but lacks fervor is lifeless. Worship that is passionate but unscriptural is fruitless. But when we worship God in both spirit and truth, it is priceless. It is only when we combine these two ingredients that our worship can truly have meaning. Is your worship unexciting? Is it passionate but pointless? Remember to combine the two basic ingredients of worship so that your soul will receive all that God has for you.

# DAY NINETY

## Sibling Rivalry

Even though Theresa and Tanya were identical twins, they were about as opposite as could be. Theresa was a tomboy who liked sports and being outside. She could be found most often wearing ragged blue jeans and tee shirts, never much worried about her outward appearance. By contrast, Tanya was the quintessential high-maintenance girl. She was constantly aware of the state of her hair, make-up and nails and had no time for the messy activities of her sister. While these two girls operated in completely different realms, their lives were often full of turmoil sparked by the jealousy and self-centeredness of children vying to be preeminent in the family pecking order. While petty bickering and squabbles may not be uncommon with younger children, their parents hoped that as the girls grew and matured, they will learn to put away their need to argue and begin to get along each other, that harmony and cooperation would eventually become the norm. Though their fights decreased over the years, old habits die hard. Sadly the girls never seemed ready to let old wounds go and build a healthy and happy relationship with the one person who should be closest to them.

As followers of Jesus, we are all God's children. Though we may have differing opinions as to how loud or long our services should be or what they should look like, we have all been brought to life from spiritual death by the same Heavenly Father. When God began His church and it reached out over the miles and the centuries, He did not envision His children wasting precious time developing and holding onto petty arguments that would only serve to divide them. His word reminds us that "since God so loved us, we also ought to love one another." (1 John 4:11) His plan has always been that His children would love each other and work together, that harmony and cooperation would be the norm. We, therefore, must grow and mature in our approach to our brothers and sisters in Christ and not allow jealousy and bickering to contaminate our minds, but build healthy and happy relationships with those who should be closest to us. Do you struggle to get along with your spiritual family members? Are you having trouble letting go of past difficulties and differences? Remember that as children of God, we will be together for eternity in the great family reunion in heaven. We must start now to be His family while here on earth as well.

# ABOUT THE AUTHOR

Ron Barnett has been in Christian ministry since 1992. Having grown up in church he has served as a Youth Pastor, Associate Pastor, and Evangelist as well as in the music ministry as a singer and musician. He is currently the Lead Pastor at Crystal Springs Assembly of God. Originally from Ohio, he makes his home in Jacksonville, FL with his wife Beth. They have been married for 19 years and have two children.

Made in the USA
Charleston, SC
28 November 2012